Luther and the Reformation

31270

LUTHER
and the Reformation

V. H. H. GREEN, D.D.
Fellow of Lincoln College, Oxford

UNIVERSITY PAPERBACKS

METHUEN & CO LTD London

© V. H. H. Green 1964
First published 1964 by
B. T. Batsford Ltd

First published as a University Paperback 1969
by Methuen & Co Ltd
11 New Fetter Lane London E.C.4

SBN 416 29770 6

Printed photolithographically by
Latimer Trend & Co Ltd
Whitstable & London

*This book is sold subject to the condition that it
shall not, by way of trade or otherwise, be lent,
re-sold, hired out, or otherwise circulated without
the publisher's prior consent in any form of
binding or cover other than that in which it is
published and without a similar condition
including this condition being imposed on the
subsequent purchaser.*

Contents

Acknowledgment

Figure 17 is reproduced by gracious permission of Her Majesty The Queen.

The Author and Publishers wish to thank the following for permission to reproduce illustrations included in this book:

The Abingdon Press for figs. 11, 18, 21, 22, 30, 33, 35.

The Bibliothèque Municipale of Arras and Messrs Photographie Giraudon for fig. 20.

Professor N. Cohn and Messrs Martin Secker and Warburg for fig. 16 (from Professor Cohn's book *The Pursuit of the Millennium*).

The Dahlem Museum, Berlin, for fig. 10.

The Devonshire Collection, Chatsworth, for fig. 8, reproduced by permission of the trustees of the Chatsworth Settlement.

The Marquess of Exeter for fig. 6, also used on the jacket of the book.

The Kunsthistorisches Museum, Vienna, for fig. 32.

The Kunstmuseum, Basel, for figs. 27 and 28.

The Lutherhalle, Wittenberg, for figs. 12 and 29.

The Mansell Collection, London, for figs. 4, 5, 9, 13, and 14.

The Trustees of the National Galleries of Scotland for fig. 25.

The Radio Times Hulton Picture Library for fig. 23.

The Earl of Radnor for fig. 31.

The Staatliche Kunsthalle, Karlsruhe, for fig. 24.

Sir Thomas Merton for fig. 19.

The Illustrations

Introduction

Few people had heard of Martin Luther before he posted the 95 theses to the door of the Castle Church at Wittenberg on October 31st, 1517; but within less than four years he had become a familiar and feared name in the universities and courts of every European country. His books were read avidly everywhere. Even in Oxford, remote from Wittenberg, John Dorne sold a dozen or so copies in 1520. The leading scholar of his time, Erasmus, commented approvingly, if with some reserve, on the stand which Luther had taken: 'I have turned over a few pages of your *Commentaries on the Psalms*', he told him, 'they please me exceedingly'. It was not, however, long before the established order in Church and State took action to stem the propagation of Luther's revolutionary ideas. His books were burned by papal order at Rome in the Piazza Navona on June 15th, 1520; bonfires blazed and smouldered with his writings in various German cities, Ingolstadt, Cologne and elsewhere, throughout the autumn and winter of 1520. The same year, or possibly somewhat later, the proctors' accounts at Cambridge included the statement 'To Dr. Nycolas, deputy Vice-chancellor, for drink and other expenses about the burning of the books of Martin Luther, 2s'. In the following April, bonfires were lit in Venice and Naples. At the same time, the Sorbonne at Paris condemned Luther's teaching, and on August 3rd, following, the Parlement of Paris proclaimed that anyone owning Luther's books was liable to a fine or imprisonment. Before the end of March, 1521, Cardinal Wolsey, Henry VIII's all-powerful minister, forbade the importation and reading of his books in England. Then, as a gesture of goodwill to the Pope and Emperor and as a sequel to the Imperial condemnation of Luther at the Diet of Worms, on May 12th a vast crowd which included Wolsey and the Archbishop of Canterbury as well as many foreign ambassadors—the King was himself ill with ague and could not attend—watched Luther's published writings burn in St. Paul's churchyard. Bishop John Fisher of Rochester, in a sermon which lasted two hours, declared that Luther 'hath stirred a mighty storm and tempest in the church'. 'Furthermore', he went on, 'he terribly thundereth against the Pope's authority, against the general councils, against the traditions and ordinances left unto us by the apostles, against the doctrines of the fathers and doctors of the church.'

What was it all about? In 1521 Luther was already 38 years old and he had a quarter of a century of life before him. To a later historian the differences between Luther and his opponents may seem relatively unimportant and the Reformation itself a less significant watershed in human history than was once thought; but there can be no doubt that Luther's revolt was a major incident in the history of the Christian Church. He had, as Bishop Fisher rightly said, 'stirred a mighty storm and tempest in the church'. He had broken the unchallenged domination of the Catholic Church, and effectively splintered its unity; by his appeal to experience and to the history of the early Church he had claimed that the Word of God in the Scriptures was the sole authority for the Christian and that 'justification by faith' was a fundamental belief. Whatever the other reformers contributed to the growth and development of Protestantism, Martin Luther was the presiding genius and initiator of the Protestant Reformation. 'Even if Christianity disappeared', Professor Butterfield has written, 'so that he survived only as a maker of myths he would still be a colossal figure—almost the greatest of the giants in modern times.'

Martin Luther must, however, be placed in his historical setting. If we are to understand the nature of what he laboured to achieve, we must reach some conclusions about the character and importance of the Reformation as well as of the social and religious order of that medieval world which it helped to bring to an end. Luther's message would have been less effective if the ground had not been prepared for it. We must glance at those features of late medieval society which were steadily transmuting it and which helped to make possible a favourable response to Luther's challenge. It is only after we have considered these problems that we can turn to the life and work of the man himself. Yet it is fair to add that the answers to these questions will only confirm the impression that few men in any age have made such a dynamic impact on the course of events. Luther fashioned the development of the Church in the centuries which followed and directly as well as indirectly influenced the faith and lives of countless Christians. The spurs of smoke which arose from so many marketplaces in 1520–1 were the omens of a religious revolution, whatever final significance we may attach to that event in the pattern of world history.

10

CHAPTER 1

Prelude to the Reformation

In the sixteenth century the men and women of western Europe experienced a major crisis, the outcome of which did much to determine the future course of world history. In its apparent causes, its outward manifestations and its final effects, the Reformation would seem to have been primarily an event in religious history. Moral, doctrinal and spiritual factors helped to bring it about. It resulted in the fragmentation of the Church and a repudiation of the long-accepted authority of the Pope of Rome, and it created deep breaches in the unity and faith of Christendom.

But it was not merely an event in the history of the Church. Just as social and political developments of a predominantly secular character had helped to bring it into being and had made possible a favourable response to the reformers' teaching, so the fracture of western Christendom, and the emergence of Protestant theology encouraged, conditioned and caused changes in the social and political climate of the sixteenth- and seventeenth-century world. The appearance of national or state churches was occasioned by, and simultaneously contributed to, the development of growing national consciousness and the growth in the authority, sometimes approaching absolutism, of the national sovereign. Religious controversy, inextricably entangled with political and economic power politics, served to foster as to fester inter-state rivalries, and to harbour war and intolerance. On the other hand, Protestant culture necessarily evoked questions relating to the obligation of the individual to obey the sovereign authority, and precipitated, if accidentally, the claim to resist the unjustified use of power and as a sequel the individual's right to share in government.

The fissiparous tendency in Protestantism, implicit in its purely scriptural basis, brought into existence many radical groups or sects, individualistic, biblical in their teaching and often perpetrating a revolutionary social teaching; they encouraged democratic developments in the churches as in the political and social life of the community. These were all consequences of which the original reformers, innately conservative in their teaching, would very likely have strongly disapproved; but they evolved from the fundamentals which they had stressed. The Protestants' repudiation of ecclesiastical authoritarianism, and their appeal to the individual enlightened by the inspired Word of God, modified as this often was by the political circumstances in which men found themselves, certainly contributed to a more radical and ultimately more liberal outlook on the world. Eventually, albeit reluctantly, the very concept of toleration itself was dragged from the welter of blood and controversy to which the split in the one Church had given rise in the sixteenth century.

Moreover the theological teaching of the reformers, stressing, as they nearly all did to a greater or lesser degree, the basic authority of the Scriptures, the doctrines of justification, election and sanctification, created what may be described as a new ethic, drawn from the Puritan idea of holiness, with its awareness of the guidance of the Holy Spirit, its concern with biblical theology and its total, at times severe and pedantic, regulation of the moral activity of the individual and the community. Whether this also helped to bring about the economic individualism characteristic of capitalistic society has been a matter of deep debate; but at least the Protestant teaching emphasised the virtues, the industry, the honesty, the sense of vocation, the obligation of duty and the sobriety which a thriving economy required. All in all the effects of the Reformation on western Europe and on those parts of the world colonised by Protestant Europeans can hardly be over-estimated, even if it is by no means easy to differentiate the political and economic development that formed its inevitable handmaid.

Nonetheless the 'modern' features of the Reformation should not be overstressed. While it may be justly regarded as a watershed in the history of European life, paradoxically the Reformation appears more and more to be the last of the great medieval movements, the sequel to Hildebrandine reform, to the monastic renaissance, to the rise of the friars and to the outbreak of the Lollard and the Hussite heresies. The Reformation did not inaugurate the modern age but rather terminated the Middle Ages. The reformers did not challenge the theological ideology fundamental to the medieval world, the Christian teaching on which they as much as their rivals founded their faith, the divine creation of the universe, the disobedience perpetrated through original sin, the redemption of the world by Jesus Christ, the Son of God, very man and very God, and the hope of eternity offered to all those whom God had accepted. They had indeed overturned the superstructure which past history had promoted, more especially the belief in the Petrine supremacy, and the sacramental and sacerdotal order which, they held, had distorted Scripture and apostolic practice. While there can be no question that this challenge was vitally signi-ficant for the future, the reformers had simply substituted one set of dogmatic ideas for another, as inelastic in their demands, as founded on revelation (and in some sense tradition), as equally binding in their moral and doctrinal teaching, in many ways as conservative and as authoritarian in their character and in a marked degree maintained by similar threats of discipline and even of force. If the reformers used the tools of textual criticism and scholarship which the humanist scholars of the late fifteenth century had brought to light, they were concerned to stem the more liberal and libertarian aspects of Renais-sance life and teaching. In other words the Reformation was in many respects a thoroughly medieval movement, backward-looking and basically suspicious of innovation and liberalism in thought and action.

The real watershed in the history of the modern world was repre-sented less by the Renaissance humanists and Protestant reformers than by the seventeenth-century scientists and eighteenth-century rationalists who, helped by economic and social change, presented a more penetrating challenge to the medieval ideology for which both reformers and their opponents almost equally stood. Yet even if we allow, and the hypothesis can be easily criticised, that the Reformation was the last of the great movements of the medieval world, the reformers in abrogating the claims of the authoritarian Church had certainly effected a major revolution in the western European's way of thinking. They had defied some of the basic beliefs that had helped to condition western Europe for some centuries past.

The medieval world was a closed society. All historical generalisations are indeed suspect, but it is safe to say that from the eleventh to the fourteenth centuries western Europe was in the main a rural community of lords and peasants, the latter dependent tillers of the soil, attached to the lord or rather to the land to a greater or lesser degree, owing him burdens or incidents of one sort or another in return for the protection and justice which he gave or was supposed to give them. There were indeed pockets of free peasantry, just as there were autonomous communes, urban societies in central and northern Italy, drawing an increasing livelihood from commerce and incipient industry. Yet the medieval world was by and large a society dominated by lordship and sustained by a coherent theological and philosophical pattern of existence, neither of which could be seriously questioned even if there was room for flexibility within the accepted boundaries of medieval thought.

The pattern of dominion was so labyrinthine as almost to defy analysis. Intelligent men were agreed that, under God, authority was vested in the temporal and spiritual heads, the Emperor (and as far as the western world went this meant the Holy Roman Emperor, for the Byzantine Empire diverged so far from the western pattern as to be omitted from consideration) and the Pope. Their jurisdictional relationship gave rise to continuous controversy, especially after a renaissance of papal power in the eleventh century, for while hardly any one doubted that both the Emperor and the Pope held their power from God, there was a considerable divergence of opinion as the extent, nature and function of such authority as each claimed. In theory the Pope was placed in an immensely stronger position, if only as a result of the scriptural texts such as St. Matthew, xvi, 18–19, and the past traditions to which the papalists could refer; the *Epistola Clementis*, for instance, recorded a supposed statement by St. Peter by which he conferred upon his successors 'the authority of binding and loosing in order that whatever he will decide upon earth, will be approved in heaven, for he will bind what must be found and he will loose what should be loosed'. The Pope held therefore both the *potestas jurisdictionis* and the *potestas ordinis*. All power properly speaking was an ecclesiastical function. '*Per me*', the Pope could quote, '*reges regnant et principes principantur.*' Precedent and argument were on the Pope's side. The Emperor, whose position was in logic (as in Scripture) so much weaker than that of the Pope and whose appeal to past history was weakened (though less so to contemporaries than to later historians) by the lack of genuine continuity which typified the story of the Holy Roman Empire, drew his strength from his geographical remoteness and the loyalty of his vassals. The authority of both Pope and Emperor was distinctively monarchical and derived from God without human mediation, albeit the college of cardinals came to elect the Pope and at long last the electoral princes the Emperor. The stratified society of western Europe was composed of many other authorities, kings, dukes, many of them in practice independent lords, only related to the Emperor by the most tenuous of ties and willing to use every available authority to weaken the *plenitudo potestatis* of the Pope to which they were inevitably subordinate. And below in kaleidoscopic variety, there were lords and sub-lords, barons, cities and bishops, all of whom depended ultimately on the acquiescence and labour of a rural peasantry and a relatively small urban proletariat.

Lordship and hierarchy, so abundantly obvious on earth and so inescapable, were an expression of the revealed truth behind all creation, the truth which ruled the universe and the serried stars and which was enshrined in Scripture and manifested through the living body of the Church. For the intelligent man in the twelfth century, as for his successor four centuries later, there was relatively little doubt about the intelligible unity of the universe. God was incontrovertibly in control, its creator, its master and its lord. His creatures had been made for His service. Their final bliss came from Him, from enjoying Him and from praising Him. Yet if He was the Lord of the Universe expecting, as earthly lords did, dues and services from all His creatures, spiritual and temporal, in return for the justice and protection He afforded them, His lordship, as was often the case with earthly lords, had not gone unchallenged. Was not rebellion as the 'sin of witchcraft'? When, how and why this happened was enfolded in the moving story of Adam and Eve. God had been defied by the Evil One, the Devil, Satan, whose lieutenants were everywhere tempting and enticing men and women to follow their master's example. We shall not easily understand the medieval world, nor indeed Martin Luther, or, for that matter, St. Paul himself, unless we realise that the universe

15

was alive with evil forces whispering, luring, deadening conscience and summoning to sin. The reality of sin, by which Luther was so much affected, was endemic in medieval culture.

But God in His goodness and love had intervened in the course of history by sending His Son to the world, to take on human flesh, to suffer and to endure and by His death on Calvary to pay on man's behalf the price of sin. While there were in the Middle Ages, as now, many varying views about the nature of Christ's atonement, by and large the interpretation was sacrificial and penal. Thomas Aquinas, perhaps not entirely representative of common opinion, insisted that the Passion affected our salvation in four ways: by merit, for the merit which Christ then acquired is transmitted to the members of the Church of which He is the head; by satisfaction, for Christ pleased God more by his passion than men displeased Him by their sins; by sacrifice, since it was a true and voluntary sacrifice well pleasing to God; and by redemption, since man, enslaved by Satan and so liable to punishment according to God's righteousness, was freed from both of these by Christ's gift of Himself. Christ paid the price to God, not to Satan. All were agreed that while baptism, penance and good works were required of men, God had ultimately triumphed over evil. Medieval theologians as much as Luther were convinced of God's mastery and lordship throughout the universe.

This breath-taking view of life, its basic soteriological mythology, offering much consolation to those burdened by the cares and evils of the world and at the same time providing such ample reserves of power for the sacerdotal order, had been entrusted by Christ to His Church to avail for the salvation of mankind. Although every baptized Christian (and this meant every man and woman in the western world) was a member of the Church, historical circumstances had largely made the Church identifiable with its ministers. The participation of the laity was passive rather than active; though many were drawn to the monastic life and to the exercise of good works. The Church, it was held, had preserved apostolic teaching, prevented the intrusion of error, eradicated heresy, safeguarded the creeds, enshrined a living tradition and was there to teach the way of life, to lead in worship and to administer discipline wherever it was needed. The priesthood had been instituted by Christ Himself, indeed He was Himself that great high priest *secundum ordinem Melchizedek*; but He had in particular entrusted the care of the flock to His disciple, St. Peter (as the text, St. John, xxi, 21f, was held to prove), and through him to every subsequent bishop of Rome. The Church was governed by bishops as the successors of the Apostles but they owed their jurisdictional power to the Pope. The divine hierarchy was mirrored in the Church as in the State by its threefold order and its manifold ministry. The Pope, in virtue of his divine appointment, was there to lead earthly kings to the throne of God, to chastise and to rebuke as well as to encourage and to support. He had the power to impose spiritual sanctions, of which excommunication was the most widely used. His authority was such that it seemed to run in the courts of heaven as well as those of earth, for in some sense, *Papa est Deus.*

The priest was thus the cornerstone of the fabric of medieval life. He celebrated the sacraments, baptized, heard confessions, gave penance and absolution and administered extreme unction. Above all else he celebrated the sacrifice of the Mass, repeating at the altar the sacrifice of Christ (though in no way detracting from the sufficiency of the Sacrifice of Calvary), a propitiation for the living and for the dead. Mass, as a medieval English writer put it, was the 'highest prayer that holy Church can devise for the salvation of the quick and the dead' when the 'priest offereth up the highest sacrifice and best offering that any heart can devise, that is, Christ, God's Son in Heaven, under the form of bread and wine'. At the words of consecration there was, it had been generally agreed since the early Middle Ages, a miraculous change in the 'substance' of the Bread and Wine, which became the Body and Blood of Christ, although the accidents remained the same. The priest, ignoble though he might be, held the power of life and death in medieval society.

The Church was then the focal-point of a predominant ideology. Its contribution to life and culture cannot be doubted. Whatever its shortcomings, it invested a world that was still barbarian and crude with deep ideals, with high standards of behaviour and with the charity, love and humanity which stemmed from the Gospel it was there to propagate. It provided a career open to talent, for the humblest-born cleric had a chance, albeit a remote one, of a cardinal's hat. It never lost sight of its basic function. It fostered learning and art, architecture and music; it gave impressive examples of courage and piety, self-sacrifice and supreme devotion. It is doubtful whether any society housed such a treasure of rich spirituality or, for all its accretions, so splendid a ceremonial and liturgy. Its devotion to the Blessed Virgin Mary and the saints enhanced the standing of women and humanised its puritanism of outlook. It was, however, severely paternal in its attitude. Castles and churches were the great buildings of the Middle Ages, epitomizing for the ordinary man the earthly and the spiritual

17

lordship and tutelage by which he was bound. The Church imposed its will by a mass of sanctions and maintained itself by a host of demands, fiscal as well as spiritual. It was the greatest property-owner in Europe and it had assimilated temporal as well as spiritual lordship.

It would not tolerate any defiance of its authority, especially in those fundamental matters where rebellion was sinful and satanic. Within the acceptable area of theological speculation there was ample opportunity for deep, penetrating and critical debate; it was within this framework that scholastic thought itself developed. There were in the early Middle Ages comparatively few challenges to the teaching of the Church; but the Albigensians represented a real threat to its doctrinal position in the late twelfth and early thirteenth century. The Church's reaction was instructive. It readily invoked the power of the State and approved force to support persuasion in preventing the spread of heterodoxy. Medieval man was therefore as much conditioned to the acceptance of a certain ideology as a modern communist, and like the communist he could not speculate or teach or act outside the conventional frontiers without danger to himself and society. The reasoning which lay behind such intolerance was similar. The modern communist believes that the dissemination of ideas critical or hostile to the Marxist-Leninist philosophy represents a social infection which can imperil the health of the whole community. The medieval theologian likewise held that a denial of the accepted ideology endangered the soul of the heretic as well as the good weal of the whole people. In general, then, medieval men and women were bound to accept that there was not merely a structure of belief that was essential to their eternal salvation, as well as to the well-being of individuals and societies, but that there also existed by divine interposition an order in society which mediated this salvation to men and women and which was empowered to impose sanctions to preserve its authority.

The late Middle Ages, however, witnessed significant developments, which prepared the ground for the reformers. The steady increase in the population of western Europe, with consequent land hunger and colonisation of the waste, prosperous farming and increased productivity came to an end, partly as a result of the Black Death (1349) and subsequent plagues. In the later Middle Ages the population declined, rentals from land decreased and there was a fall in agrarian produce as well as in manufactures. This helped to hasten the transmutation of the feudal fabric of society. The peasantry in the main profited from these trends since prices remained static or even declined whilst

18

wages, as a result of the shortage of labour, tended to rise. Economic and political factors furthered the process of commutation, enabling the peasant to free himself of all but his tenurial dues. His personal freedom and comparative prosperity gave the peasant a sense of his importance in society, and may consequently have made him more resentful than he had been of the fiscal demands of the Church which, now that the lay landlord had become more remote, was the more immediate reminder of the passing feudal order. Equally he may well have been readier than he had once been to emancipate himself spiritually (as he had to some extent done economically) from ecclesiastical dominion, if the opportunity for doing so presented itself.

The landowners themselves had been seriously affected by the fall in their revenues which declining rentals represented, more especially as they seemed unable at least in western Germany to take adequate steps to counter this trend by raising rents or reviving services. Some, as for instance the Teutonic Order of Knights, never effectively recovered from the agrarian depression. Economic factors certainly helped to make the nobles more dependent than they had been formerly on the territorial princes of Germany whose authority was steadily increasing; and for economic reasons both looked with hungry eyes on the extensive properties in land, buildings and treasure of the Church.

In the towns rather a different situation prevailed. They too were inevitably affected by the recession in trade; but the improved standard of living led to a sustained demand for goods. Their economic conditions may well have favoured their growing importance in the life of fifteenth-century Europe. At Frankfort, for example, the price of goods, especially of cereals, was declining before 1470; but began to rise slowly and steadily in subsequent years. Wages on the other hand remained more or less unchanged. The town workers were therefore in relatively comfortable circumstances until the last few decades of the fifteenth century. The increasing importance of an educated class of burghers sponsored a growing dislike of ecclesiastical power and privilege which they regarded as the remnants of a discredited feudal lordship. In some towns the middle-class burghers and the proletariat were jealous of the property and position of the greater merchants and of the Church with which they were closely aligned. Economic developments, and if what has just been written refers more particularly to western and central Germany much the same picture could be drawn roughly throughout western Europe, may well have created fertile soil for anti-ecclesiastical movements, even if they did not themselves precipitate the Reformation or indeed call it into being. ⟵——

The political developments of the later Middle Ages also worked towards a diminution in the institutional power of the Church and the weakening of its pretensions. The assimilation of the recently re-discovered works of Aristotle led to the acceptance of the belief that the state was a natural, organic development and that the ultimate source of its power and authority was to be found in its citizens. In the fourteenth century William of Occam severely criticised the papal claim to temporal dominion, and Marsiglio of Padua would have excluded the clergy from all but purely spiritual functions, holding that the Church was no more than a mystical sodality of believers. Moreover the canonists were themselves hinting that authority over the Church was vested, not solely in the Pope as the successor of Peter, but in the *populus christianus*, the *ecclesia Christi*, a notion that received fuller and more definite expression in the conciliar movement at the start of the fifteenth century and which was fundamentally and diametrically opposed to the long-held belief about the *plenitudo potestatis* of the Pope.

The revival of the Holy Roman Empire by the house of Luxemburg in the early years of the fourteenth century had served to indicate the weakness of the Imperial institution, and under the Hapsburgs who acceded to the Imperial throne in 1438 the futility and executive impotence of the Imperial title was further underlined: the reality of the Hapsburg power came from the family's own territorial estates and the dynastic marriages which the Hapsburg emperors arranged to subsidise and extend their influence. The Holy Roman Emperor was effectively the first of the German princes and of the other diverse authorities, dukes, princes, bishops, imperial cities, who were repre-sented in the estates of the Imperial Diet and who made up the diversified conglomeration of powers which constituted the Holy Roman Empire. The German princes had themselves taken every advantage of the weak and unreformed Empire to develop their own autonomy; and had in many respects achieved virtual independence. If theoretically the Emperor could be regarded as having in temporal matters an authority similar to that of the Pope, a reduction in his power conversely weakened the papal estate. Yet, gimcrack and the worse for wear as the Empire appeared to be at the end of the fifteenth century, the glamour of the Imperial title remained.

Elsewhere national monarchies had developed in France, England and the Spanish kingdoms, each in its turn winning greater power over the Church and church appointments to the exclusion of papal influence. Even in Italy itself there had been a real delimitation of papal prestige as the Papacy, pressed by circumstances, tended to become one among the disputing Italian states. The rise of national consciousness for the first time made apparent the Italian character of the curia. All this was assisted by the greater part that laymen played in affairs of state as in local administration. The development of princely power, itself a threat to the oecumenical authority of the Pope, had been paralleled by an improvement in and extension of the facilities available for the education of the laity. An increasing number of laymen were doing jobs in government, in diplomacy and local administration which had previously been the monopoly of the clergy. Many had a legal training and, fortified by Roman law, were not slow to challenge the teaching of the canonists and to encroach upon ecclesiastical privileges.

The Church, confronted with a rapidly changing situation, failed to adapt itself effectively to the needs of the developing society. It was indeed placed at an immense disadvantage by its own history in the later Middle Ages. From 1305 to 1370 the Papacy had had its headquarters at a papal enclave inside France at the fair city of Avignon. The Avignonese popes discerned something of their true function, seeking to act as international arbiters, but their cosmopolitan character was in the view of their contemporaries sadly tarnished by their close alignment with France. Moreover their absence from Rome involved them in constant war in Italy. The growing efficiency of the papal secretariat, the expenses of a luxurious curia, the heavy cost of war all gravely overburdened the papal finances and created demands for money which further exacerbated the national states. The Papacy's return from Avignon to Rome gave rise to the scandal of a disunited Christendom, for from 1378 to 1415 two popes, and from 1409 three, claimed that they were the true successors of St. Peter and they all seemed to disprove the validity of their claims to apostolic authority by the mundane character of their pontificates. The restoration of the unity of the Roman Papacy accomplished by the General Council which met at Constance did not mean a revival of its brightness. The Council of Constance which had ended the schism condemned heretical movements (in the persons of the Lollards and Hussites) without effectively removing the abuses which had been criticised to an increasing extent by vigilant churchmen. Indeed abuses and corruption in the Church, how far worse than those of an earlier period, if now more publicised, it is impossible to know, constituted a grave scandal

21

and in the long run afforded fertile propaganda for humanists and reformers. 'We leave it to you to judge', Pius II wrote reprovingly to one of his cardinals in 1460, Rodrigo Borgia (the future Pope Alexander VI), 'if it is becoming in one of your position to toy with girls, to pelt them with fruits . . . and, neglecting study, to spend the whole day in every kind of pleasure.' The popes themselves, fearful of the threat to their authority that a general council represented, eventually crushed the conciliar movement and halted or disregarded the demand for reform.

The fifteenth-century popes concentrated their attention to an increasing extent on strengthening their hold on their Italian possessions, which now provided a far greater proportion of their revenue than in the past, thus countering the reduced income that they received from the Church as a whole. Papal revenues had been so adversely affected by the Great Schism that curial officials were obliged to explore new sources of revenue. The popes of the later fifteenth and early sixteenth century established colleges of offices, either sinecures or with a very limited function, which were sold to increase the papal income. It has been calculated that in 1520 some 2,000 of these offices were venal, 'representing an invested capital of about $2\frac{1}{2}$ million gold florins and an annual interest of about 300,000 gold florins'. The existence of this curial bureaucracy constituted a major stumbling-block to any scheme of church reform. At the same time there was a marked increase in the income drawn from dispensations and indulgences. The exploitation of the newly-discovered alum mines at Tolfa added further to the papal income; and the Pope subsequently sought to create a monopoly by forbidding the import of Turkish alum and by restricting through the Medici bank the output from the Neapolitan mines at Ischia, though without great success. Papal finances recovered, but at a price. The popes and those who advised them may well have regarded the consolidation and extension of their authority in Italy as an essential pre-requisite both for financial stability and for the effective execution of their true Petrine function; but even the most devout Catholic could not deny the deterioration in the character of the curia and the seeming secularisation that accompanied it.

The Church's failure to capitalise the good will and the devotion of Christians which, for all that has been said, was clearly not lacking, illustrated its striking inability to discern the signs of the times. There was a genuine desire to cut through the superfluities of the liturgy, to by-pass the aridity of theologian exposition and to eliminate the atrophy which afflicted the secular and religious life of the Church. The popularity of mystical writings and of works of devotion written for lay people exemplifies the spiritual life of the fifteenth century.

It would be fair to say that the establishment had been sapped from within. There had been developments in the field of scholastic learning which certainly harboured potential change. The thirteenth century had seen a great revolution, precipitated by the newly-rediscovered works of Aristotle, as a result of which the dominant Augustinianism had been significantly modified by Thomas Aquinas and his followers. Thomist ideas were themselves challenged in the ensuing period, more especially by Duns Scotus and William of Occam. Although there had been some attempt, notably by the Englishman, Thomas Bradwardine, to revive Augustinianism, the prevailing academic current brought theology and philosophy under the control of nominalist teachers who drew their original inspiration from Occam. The nominalists discarded the Thomist synthesis of faith and reason. 'This I say', Occam had declared, 'that no universal is existent in any way whatsoever outside the mind of the knower.' If this was so then the process of knowledge was intuitional and metaphysical knowledge unattainable. Any knowledge of the extra-mental universe was virtually impossible. This meant that truths of natural religion were incapable of demonstration. 'We hold', Occam commented in a discussion of the soul and its attributes, 'these three truths by faith only'. Man was forced to accept that which faith and revelation provided for him. If Occam clearly opened the way to absolute scepticism, he at once closed it by stressing the arbitrary will, the sovereignty and the power of God.

Nominalism is a difficult philosophy to interpret and to understand; nor is there universal agreement as to its significance; but it radically changed the climate of academic thinking, acting as acid on the Christian aristotelianism of the previous century with its 'conception', as Professor Knowles has put it, 'of an ordered, interlocking universe which in its turn was permeated by, and dovetailed into, the economy of supernatural grace'. Through their assertion that the truths of natural reason may not be demonstrated and depend entirely on a revelation that springs from the arbitrary will of God, the nominalists alternatively prepared the way for scepticism or an extreme and unreasoning fideism. Further their neglect of tradition made possible an ultimate reliance on Scripture alone. There can be little doubt that they contributed to important developments in the realm of logic and of mechanics but their predominance in university teaching not merely reduced the standing of theology but may well have helped to foster the general atmosphere of uncertainty that prevailed at the end of the fifteenth century. Certainly the rarefied air the schoolmen breathed helped to remove further the contact between theology and the common man, and stimulated both the study of the mystics and the reading of pious works of simple, scriptural devotion.

In one respect the Church may be said to have come to terms with contemporary developments; but in so doing it helped its own undoing. Apparently more and more an Italian institution, the Papacy could not disregard the revival of art and literature taking place so close to its borders. Popes soon became the patrons of the new humanism, tolerating to a surprising degree ideas that were superficially pagan, epicurean and cynical. Lorenzo Valla and his colleagues aimed penetrating darts at the court which patronised them and the faith it held. When humanism went further afield, its critical potentialities became even more plainly apparent. Erasmus, its major prophet, did not merely thrust scholasticism out of doors but by his editions of the early Fathers and of the Greek Testament provided the instruments which could be easily utilised to challenge the teaching and practice of the Church. Nor was this all. He and his fellow humanists writing on the eve of the printing press made available for a wide public satirical writings which held monks and clerics, miracles and shrines, in ridicule and disrepute. The power and position of the clerical order had been undermined some time before Luther enrolled as a student at the University of Erfurt. As early as 1463 Pope Pius II, appealing for support for his crusade against the Turks, commented bluntly that 'the priesthood is a laughing stock, the very name of cleric is an infamy. They say we live for pleasure, hoard up money, serve ambition, sit on fat mules or pedigree horses, spread out the fringes of our cloaks and go about the city with fat cheeks under our red hats and ample hoods: that we breed dogs for hunting, spend freely upon players and parasites, but nothing in defence of the faith. Nor is it all a lie. Many of the Cardinals and other courtiers do all these things and, to speak the truth, the luxury and extravagance of our Curia is excessive.'

Moreover, the appearance of heresy and the continued and growing strength of anti-clericalism no doubt contributed to all this. Anti-clericalism, an endemic feature of any society dominated by a priesthood, was in many ways a spontaneous outburst against a privileged order from which men could not, without spiritual and other penalties, free themselves. It was fostered by the Church's demands for money, in the form of tithes and fees, and by the oft apparent contrast between the lives of the clergy and the teaching of the Gospel which they were supposed to proclaim. Except for the Albigensians, heresy for the most part had so far been sporadic and in the main individualistic. Then at the end of the fourteenth century the Lollards in England and the Hussites in Bohemia made a resolute challenge to the existing order in the Church. The texture of their thought may still have been intrinsically medieval. The Lollard leader, John Wyclif, was an Oxford don frustrated by his failure to win papal preferment and royal patronage, and the originator of the Bohemian movement, John Hus, may have been primarily concerned with expressing Bohemian dislike of German influence and domination; but Lollard and Hussite teaching to a greater or lesser extent cut at the roots of Catholic orthodoxy and government. It is hardly surprising that at a later date Luther came to see in Hus an earlier exponent of his teaching; though closer acquaintance with his work would have revealed important divergences. The Lollards ceased to be an effective force within 50 years of Wyclif's death; the Hussites were very much reduced in strength. Their conflict with the Church had been, however, as seminal as it was lengthy. The Lollards were imprisoned and burned, but Lollard tradition and teaching did not completely die out, especially in the north of England. The Bohemian heretics, divided among themselves, had been subdued only by bloody war; but the movement lived on and filtered through to other parts of central and eastern Europe. The western world was aware to an extent that it had never been before of the challenge and danger of heresy.

It is indeed plain that towards the end of the Middle Ages there was a current of dissatisfaction with organised religion. Much of this was incoherent and indeed inarticulate, and arose from self-interest and resentment of the dominance of the Church as an institution. There was no effective challenge to the fundamentals of belief, for it was not a sceptical age albeit there was an element of anxiety and a lack of assurance discernible in certain circles. All in all it was indeed a fideistic era, outwardly manifested in its splendid new churches, in its books of devotion, in its mystical writings, in its vocations, in the treasury of ordinary religion, in the prayers, wishes and hopes that illuminated many a human testament. There were few signs of any real demand for doctrinal reformation. Yet the winds of change had clouded the fifteenth-century sky. If an outstanding personality should make a prophetic challenge to the existing order, the signs

25

suggested that he might receive a favourable response. If it is a truism to say that in Martin Luther the hour and the man had met, it is difficult to deny that here was a personality who left an imperishable mark upon the age in which he lived, splintered the unity of Christian Europe and destroyed the domination of the Roman Church.

CHAPTER 2

Luther's Early Life and Education

1485-1512

Martin Luther was descended from a long line of free peasant proprietors, but he was educated within town walls and consequently absorbed an urban culture and outlook. Yet he was basically a man of the people introduced by time and circumstances into social groupings different from those in which he had been brought up. His physique, his shrewdness, the occasional crudity of his language were in part an inheritance from his Thuringian peasant ancestors but equally they characterised the industrial workers to whom his father came from the countryside subsequent to Martin's birth at the small Saxon town of Eisleben on November 10th, 1483. His father, Hans Luther, as a younger son had decided to see whether he could better himself as a copper miner in the town. If Martin's later comments are to be trusted, life was often hard in his early years. He remembered vividly the picture of his mother with wood on her back, availing herself of the customary privilege that permitted the peasants and workers to bring fuel from the communal forest. But, unlike his brother, a drunken good-for-nothing, Hans prospered. He became a respectable member of the middle class and, by the time that Martin was eight years old, he was serving on municipal committees at the town of Mansfeld, where he had moved the year after Martin was born. He owned his own house. He became a joint lessee of mines and furnaces. When in 1507 his son, recently ordained to the priesthood, celebrated his first Mass, Hans gave the monastery 20 florins. He was indeed a self-made man, rather dominating and determined, on occasions passionate, yet withal affectionate and kind.

Martin's early upbringing seems to have been conventional enough. It has been argued that the harsh punishments which he, with most others of his age, experienced during childhood formed traumatic experiences which left a permanent mark on his sensitive personality. There is no real evidence that this was so, but he was evidently a boy of strong feeling upon whom his everyday environment made a deep impress. He imbibed, and never lost, the religious mythology of his peasant background. The man who so acutely criticised the existing order of church government and was able to formulate new and penetrating doctrinal propositions believed all his life in demons and in the spiritual powers of darkness. His mother suffered from the attentions of a neighbouring witch to such an extent that 'she felt she ought to treat her with great deference and propitiate her, for she caused such agony to her children that they screamed as if they were at death's door'. Evil spirits disturbed the weather, ruined the crops and brought sickness to man and beast; men were drowned in the river Elbe (which passed through Wittenberg) by their agency. The universe was the scene of constant strife between God and the Devil, and their respective agents. If Christ was ultimately victorious, had indeed already triumphed, yet the Christian life was a continuous and losing struggle. To the fear evoked by his father's anger Luther had to add the alarm created by God's wrath. 'He who quivers at every word of his father and mother', he wrote later in a sermon, 'for the remainder of his existence will fear a rustling leaf', and a rustling leaf could be a manifestation of divine displeasure. 'We are not afraid for every breath of God, and we stand upright, and yet we panic and run away from a harmless dry leaf! At such a rustling a leaf assumes the form of the Wrath of God, and the whole world where a little before we swaggered in our pride appears shrivelled and small.'

His schooling calls for little comment. He went first to the Latin school at Mansfeld, then for a year at the age of 14 to a school taught by the Brethren of the Common Life at the populous, busy city of Magdeburg and finally to an academy at Eisenach, a small town pleasantly situated in a rich agricultural district where his relatives still farmed. It is easy to suppose that he enjoyed the demands of learning, though he may have resented the discipline which accompanied it. At least in later life he kept in touch with one of his teachers, urging the Elector of Saxony to grant him a pension. 'Here', as Melanchthon later put it, 'he completed the study of grammar', a tedious discipline under medieval conditions, preparatory to entering a university.

'Martinus Ludher ex Mansfelt' matriculated at the University of Erfurt in May, 1501. He was then 18 years old, perhaps a little older than some of his contemporaries, with an adequate allowance from his father who had paid his fees in advance, and endowed with considerable intellectual ability. Although Erfurt was affected by something like an economic depression during Luther's time, it was a prosperous city of fine buildings. The university had been founded in 1397 and enjoyed a good reputation. Luther like many of his fellow students lived at a university hall of residence, in his case that of St. George. University life was there, as it has always been, a strange blend of the serious and the comic, the improper and the pious. If some of Luther's contemporaries were hard-working, conscientious students, others were idle, undisciplined and lusty, drawn to beer, brothels and brawls. The old Luther recalled some of the more unedifying features of university life, but the charge of debauchery made against him by his detractors was founded on insubstantial evidence. If he was neither then or later unready to swill heady draughts of wine or beer, the pursuit of knowledge and the practice of dialectic formed the staple ingredients in his life. He did not easily forget the ceremony of initiation which inaugurated his career at the university.

What did Luther study during his years in that provincial Saxon town? Later in life he attacked remorselessly the scholastic method, more especially the neo-Aristotelian thought, of his university teachers; but it is impossible to doubt the impact which it made on his impressionable mind at the time. The University of Erfurt was by late

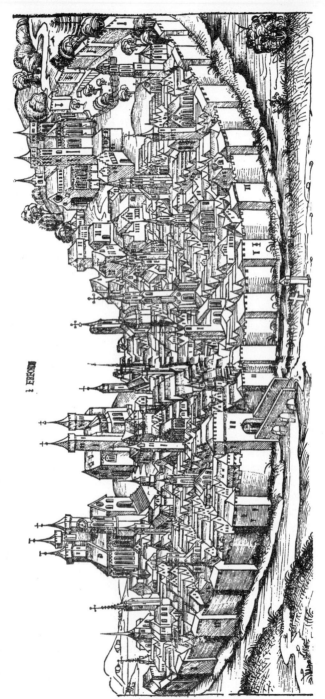

1 Erfurt. From Schedel, 'Weltchronik', 1493

medieval standards the centre of modern studies. Its professors held fast to the nominalistic scholastic methodology of the fourteenth-century writers, William of Occam and his more recent exponents, notably Gabriel Biel of Tübingen. The university's Rector, Jodocus Trutvetter, had written several textbooks on logic and another lecturer, Bartholomew Arnoldi von Usingen, was the author of a short natural history replete with neo-Aristotelian learning. Initially Luther was not, however, concerned with the bleak heights of nominalist learning. He underwent a rigorous training in logic and syllogistic method, first in logical formulae and propositions as categorised in the *Summulae logicales* of Petrus Hispanus and then in the technique of demonstration and proof, founded on the *Analytics* of Aristotle.

This training, which had severe limitations, was very necessary for the intellectual exercises, debates or disputations in which all university students had to participate. It equipped the student with rules and formulae which enabled him to argue cogently within the identifiable field of medieval scholasticism; medieval argument was not unlike an intricate game of chess, a penetrating intellectual exercise and a training for the mind but in itself devoid of contact with the realities of existence. It provided the inquirer with the tools and instruments with which he could utilise best the knowledge at his disposal. Knowledge itself, consisting in the main of set texts, commentaries and systematic encyclopaedia, received but not empirical, rested as a super-structure on strata of classified logical formulae. Within its recognised frontiers, it could be an exciting, even a thrilling pastime, but equally it could be, and often was for the dull student, an arid and tedious study. Occasionally students ventured to lighten the heavy load of scholastic disputation by facetious interpolations. Luther remembered that they once discussed at Erfurt the problem as to why St. Dominic was represented with threatening fingers and St. Francis with out-stretched hands; one student interjected that Dominic was supposed to be saying: 'O Francis, what wicked chaps you have in your order!', and to this Francis was replying: 'What can I do about it?' In fact, while the scholastic method may have been an excellent exercise for a keen mind, it discouraged experiment and in practice made almost impossible any research into matters which lay outside the accepted syllabus or were out of sympathy with the established ideology.

In spite of the forceful way in which Luther later repudiated the scholastic method, there can be little doubt that he owed much to the mental training or gymnastics to which he had to submit

2   Luther as an Augustinian Friar, aged 37
From an engraving by Lucas Cranach, 1520

his mind at school and university. It developed his extraordinarily capacious memory. It enabled him to become one of the arch-controversialists of his time, giving him the capacity for detecting the weak points in his opponents' arguments and for presenting a clear and logical presentation of his position. Although he was later to attack scholasticism as word play and sophistry, he never denied that logic was an essential ingredient in education or that logical argument was of assistance in unravelling the true meaning of human history and scriptural truth. The man of feeling never discarded the apparatus of the mental training which he sought to abrogate. Without it his theology would undoubtedly have been the poorer.

The study of logic was itself the preliminary to the study of philosophy and theology. It is difficult enough even now to simplify and explain the corpus of fifteenth-century nominalist thought, in part because of the comparatively little headway that has been made into late medieval thought by modern research workers. Luther's basic intellectual nutrition during these years was Occamist, in the sense that German nominalism, of which Gabriel Biel was the leading representative, stemmed ultimately from the teaching of the fourteenth-century Franciscan English scholar, William of Occam. Occam, and those who followed him, had effectively fractured the careful synthesis of faith and reason, of theology and philosophy, which Thomas Aquinas had put together in the previous century in his *Summa Theologica*. They held that human and divine knowledge constituted two separate provinces rather than the single empire that Aquinas had created. Human knowledge is the result, they asserted, of verifiable experience, and it consists of individual entities and facts which exist in and by themselves. It is possible to deduce their relationship to each other by means of syllogistic logic. Divine knowledge, theology, cannot be known in this sort of way. Indeed by ordinary rational definition it can hardly be described as knowledge. It is incapable of verification. Divine knowledge cannot be ascertained in the same way that human knowledge can be. God may not be 'known' as everyday experience can be known. Although the older philosophy, that usually known as realism, continued to have its defenders, the nominalists had captured the intellectual fortresses of fifteenth-century Europe.

Such being its presuppositions, nominalism might have seemed to open the way to philosophic doubt and theological scepticism; but in practice it did not do so. Paradoxically doubt and scepticism would have brought about the destruction of nominalism itself, since its negative force was countered by the stress which its advocates laid on the sovereignty of God, will and faith. No fifteenth-century theologian could possibly have followed its implications to an ultimate conclusion without endangering society and his own immortal soul by perpetrating heretical views. The nominalist might readily speculate but his speculative impulses had to be confined within an ideological framework the frontiers of which he dare not cross. He was thus able to resolve the apparent dichotomy between verifiable knowledge and theological truth by stressing the necessity of faith and the arbitrary sovereignty of God. God's existence was as axiomatic as the notions of heaven and hell. But God was absolutely free, at liberty to save or condemn those whom He willed. Men could not be properly said to merit salvation, let alone to earn it by works or charity. They could only believe that salvation was a matter of faith. There was no *absoluta necessitas* about human salvation. Yet equally the nominalist philosopher readily believed that God has decreed the way of salvation which the Church preaches. Thus while he appeared to reject the ultimate need for justification by good works in that he held that God could, if He wished, save men by faith, yet in practice he did not deny that good works were pleasing to God. He certainly did not understand faith in the sense that the Protestant reformers were to construe it.

Nonetheless, Luther's mind was impregnated by nominalist concepts. The university courses which he followed at Erfurt fertilised the soil in which his own particular doctrines were to grow. He travelled a long way with the nominalists, more especially in their insistence on the sovereign liberty of God; but he was to insert into their metaphysical discussion the pressing issue of personal salvation and man's acceptance by God. Occam had taught that God need not have willed justification by works but appeared to have done so; Luther insisted that God was here and now free to choose whom He willed, quite irrespective of human merit. The nominalist discussion was largely academic. It excited men's minds but it did not touch their souls. Significant as Luther's indebtedness to nominalist thinking was to be, he transformed, indeed metamorphosed it into a recognisably different theology, which was centred around the redemptive work of Christ.

This was, of course, what was to happen in the future. During his early years at Erfurt he followed conscientiously the courses prescribed by the university authorities, outwardly the serious-minded undergraduate of his or any other age. He graduated a bachelor in 1502 and three years later became a master, having been placed second among 17 candidates. It was the happy culmination of long years of intellectual drudgery. 'What grandeur and splendour', he recalled nostalgically, 'there was when one received the master's degree! They came with flaming torches and presented them. I think that no earthly joy could be compared to it.' What visions of the future passed through the newly fledged master's mind as the torches spluttered at this first great moment of his life?

His father hoped that he would be a lawyer. Hans Luther could well be proud of himself and of his son. He supposed that a man of Martin's gifts trained in the law would rise even higher in the social scale. It was therefore with consternation that he learned that his son had decided to discard his intended profession and become an Augustinian friar. What was the reason for a change less astonishing in the sixteenth century than it would be now? A well-attested account relates that young Luther, returning to Erfurt from a visit to Mansfeld on July 2nd, 1505, was overtaken by a sudden violent summer thunderstorm. As he neared the little village of Stotternheim there was a bright flash of lightning and so loud a peal of thunder, all so close, that he was flung to the ground in an agony of apprehension. In his fear he promised that if God saved him he would become a monk. 'Dear St. Anne [the patron saint of miners]', he prayed, 'I will become a monk.' It was a vow forced from him, he asserted later, '*terrore et agone mortis subitae circumvallatus*', by the fear of sudden death. 'Divine providence', Crotus Rubeanus wrote to him on October 31st, 1519, 'had an eye to this when, coming back from a visit to your parents, you were flung to the ground by a flash of celestial lightning as another Paul, before the town of Erfurt, and so was brought about your grievous disappearance from our company, within the walls of the Augustinian Friary', but others have suggested that a wound in his leg, the subsequent bleeding and fear of sudden death, acted as a stimulus to his vow. There is, however, nothing which makes the story of Luther in the thunderstorm unlikely. Luther, like other men of similar nature, often interpreted the events of his life in terms of a providential purpose. He cannot have forgotten St. Paul's experience on the Damascus road. The awe-compelling nature of the supreme Deity directing his thunderbolts at His intended victim would have seemed an explicable concept to an early sixteenth-century Christian.

Equally it was a less sudden decision than the episode might seem to suggest. He resented his father's attempt to dominate his life and to push him into a career which he had selected for him. When Francis of Assisi made his act of renunciation he is reported to have said, 'I say no more father Pietro di Bernardone but our father in heaven'. In similar fashion Luther's decision to become a friar may be interpreted as an act of personal independence. He did not tell his father of his final decision until he was behind the friary walls. Hans Luther did not easily forgive or forget what he may justifiably have thought to be a dereliction of duty. 'Don't you know that it is written, "Thou shalt honour thy father and thy mother?"', he shouted across the table, possibly stimulated by the liquid refreshment that he had consumed, at the feast given by Friar Martin to celebrate his first Mass. It seems to have been on this occasion that Hans questioned the validity of the vision which had brought his son to the monastery door: 'I trust that it was no illusion and trick of Satan.' Luther did not quickly forget the scene. 'It drove roots into my heart, as though God were speaking through your mouth', he wrote in the dedication to his father of his little book *On Monastic Vows*. Fundamentally Luther was a man of independent mind. He escaped one sort of discipline to embrace another which was to be eventually far more repugnant to him.

There was, however, nothing very absurd or unusual in the choice that Luther had made. The friar and the monk, the priest and the clerk were a part and parcel of the social scene. Few intelligent men can have passed through adolescence and early manhood without wondering whether they had a vocation to the sacred order. The contemporary Church almost certainly appeared less corrupt to them than it has done to its later critics and historians; they had not yet the advantage of having been told by publicists in what way it had betrayed its ideals. The cardinal in rich purple silk was the colleague of the friar living a life of Christ-like renunciation. Luther never forgot the emaciated figure of the Prince of Anhalt who had become a friar whom he had seen begging in the streets of Magdeburg.

The Augustinian Friars, of which Martin became a member, were a flourishing house, who played a vigorous part in the religious and intellectual life of Erfurt. Originally incorporated by Pope Innocent IV in 1243, the order numbered 2,000 chapters by the fifteenth century. Moreover the original austerity of the Friars' rule of life had been in part restored by reforms passed in the earlier fifteenth century. Some 30 houses of the Saxon-Thuringian province of the order, including that at Erfurt, had been brought to a stricter observance of the rule by their Vicar-General, Andreas Proles, in 1477. His successor, John Staupitz, was a shrewd and sensible man who possessed deep spiritual perception and in time became Luther's loyal friend. Undoubtedly the Augustinians' reputation for strictness must have been a powerful factor in attracting the youthful graduate. He would abandon the study of the law, arid and mundane, to embrace the spirit of the Gospel. It is hardly surprising that the Epistle to the Galatians, with its profound contrast between the law and the spirit, was later to have so great an influence over him. 'I am wedded to it; it is my Katie von Bora', he declared. He could not foresee when he was admitted to the cloister on July 17th, 1505, that the law of religion was to prove as hateful as the law of the world which he had now abandoned.

Twelve years elapsed before Luther took the action which eventually led to his discarding his monastic vows. If we were to believe Luther's own later account of these years, it would seem that they were misspent, a harsh and unrewarding period which ultimately revealed the vanity and hypocrisy of the monastic ideal. The process of disillusion was, however, very slow. His initial enthusiasm carried him through the early period of his novitiate. 'I know from my own experience, and from that of many others, how mute and quiet the Devil usually is during one's first years as a priest or monk.' He

36

embraced the rules of his order with unstinted zeal. 'I had no other thoughts than to observe my rule.' He would be the first to suffer the humiliations which connoted the sacrifice of self. He worked at the most menial of tasks, such as cleaning out the privy, and readily bore the begging sack. 'I was a good monk', he recalled in 1533, 'and kept strictly to my order, so that I could say that if the monastic life could get a man to heaven, I should have entered.' When he fasted, he did so with unrelenting rigour. He subdued the temptations of the flesh with remorseless mortification. He trained himself to a life of austerity, letting his imagination absorb the privations and devotions of the early saints. 'I used to picture such a saint, who would live in the desert and abstain from food and drink and exist on a few vegetables and roots and cold water.' He studied with meticulous industry, dredging ever deeper the tomes of scholastic learning, impregnating the memory with a stock of quotations from the Scriptures and patristic writers. A Catholic who knew Luther at this time told Matthew Flacius Illyricus in 1543 that 'Martin Luther lived a holy life among them, observed the Rule most meticulously, and studied diligently.'

It is impossible to doubt that this was so, but in his ardour and scrupulosity zeal sometimes outran discretion. Spiritual pride is one of the besetting temptations of the religious. Martin Luther found it difficult to forget himself, possibly because he was too consciously concerned with his own salvation. It was doubtful whether he was by nature fitted to the life of self-abnegation which he had imposed on himself. Throughout life he was the victim of deep mental and spiritual depression. In such low moods he found it easy to imagine that the Devil and his myrmidons were waiting to lure him to temptation. Constipation and asceticism nourished a vivid imagination. His later life showed that he enjoyed good food and drink, and that he found physical satisfaction in his marriage. He had powers of leadership which could not be readily subordinated to the self-effacement of monastic order.

It was, however, some time before he became aware of his failure to achieve a state of spiritual harmony. His natural abilities soon brought him to the forefront of his order. In the summer of 1506 he became a fully-professed friar: 'I was congratulated . . . by the prior, convent and father confessor, so that I was now like an innocent child who had just come forth pure from baptism'. Although he was most interested in academic theology, he clearly possessed administrative skill which was put to the service of his house. In October, 1516, he told Prior Lang: 'I require two scribes or secretaries. I spend almost all my time writing letters, so that I am not sure whether I am repeating what I have said before. I am lecturer at the convent, reader during meals. I am also called from day to day to preach in the parish church, act as regent of studies at the convent and subvicar, which means prior of eleven convents, have to gather the fish at Leitzkau, administer the affairs of Herzberg at Torgau, lecture on Paul, edit my lectures on the Psalms, and besides am burdened with writing letters which, as I have said, takes up much the greater part of my time. I have insufficient time for the prayers in the breviary or for saying Mass. In addition to all that, I have to fight against the temptations of the world, the flesh and the devil.' Friar Martin was then a mature man of 33 whose academic studies had already won him a considerable reputation.

He had so far spent the greater part of his life in either Erfurt or Wittenberg, but once, probably in 1510, he had been a member of a deputation despatched by his order to Rome. The houses of the stricter tradition wished to prevent an anticipated absorption of their laxer brethren into a projected union of all monasteries of the order. Twenty years elapsed before Luther described the impact the holy city made on him, but it is doubtful whether his reactions were as forceful at the time. He may well have found the contrast between the world that he knew so well and the ostentation and laxity of papal Rome bewildering and perhaps horrifying. The impressions that he received may have opened his mind to the sins of the hierarchy. This was, however, the experience of many a conscientious and holy cleric in the Middle Ages. The visit to Rome was only made later to fit into the Protestant polemic. If his travels in Italy made him critical of the secular standards of the contemporary Church, there is no reason to suppose that he returned to Saxony a disillusioned or disappointed man.

He was above all and throughout his life was to remain a university professor. While he was at Erfurt he had ample opportunity for study; under the supervision of John Paltz and John Nathin he absorbed current nominalist theology. After the completion of his preliminary course the brother went forward to theological studies which after three years earned him the title of lector with the right to instruct in the monastic school. Two further years of study brought the degree of sententiarius which allowed him to lecture on the *Sentences* of Peter Lombard. Finally the candidate for academic honours was awarded the *licentia magistralis* or doctorate. Luther's preferment to the highest degree was comparatively rapid and a tribute to his learning. In the autumn of 1508 his order sent him from Erfurt to the little town of Wittenberg to lecture in the faculty of arts on the *Nicomachean*

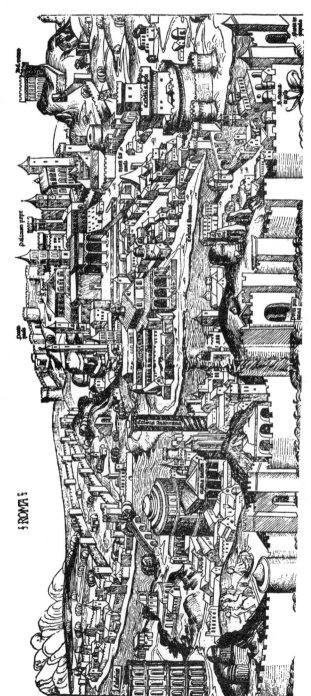

3 Rome. *From Schedel, 'Weltchronik', 1493*

Ethics of Aristotle, evidently to reinforce the tutorial staff of the newly-founded university there. After a stay of less than a year he resumed his studies at Erfurt where he remained until he was summoned back to Wittenberg in 1511.

This was the start of his long connection with the town and university which lasted until his death in 1546. Wittenberg seems to have been a small, rather dull and uninteresting place which had won the affection of the reigning Elector of Saxony. He had rebuilt his castle, which stood on its western outskirts, and decorated it with new frescoes. He had also reconstructed the collegiate church of All Saints which he intended, together with the Augustinian friary, to form the basis of a newly-founded university, which might challenge his cousin Duke George's university at Leipzig. The Electorate of Saxony had a long history, and early possessed in practice autonomous power. In 1485 it had been divided between two branches of the reigning house of Wettin, the duchy passing to Duke George and the electorate to his cousin, Frederick. Frederick was a bluff, shrewd, straightforward prince who followed the contemporary fashion of patronising art and literature. It was behaviour becoming to a prince which ministered equally to his vanity and his interest, and enhanced his reputation in the world at large. The little University of Wittenberg, granted an Imperial charter on July 6th, 1502 and approved by papal decree, became his cherished child. Under his patronage the dreary town of Wittenberg was to become an academic centre, and Luther its most distinguished professor. It says much for the Elector's devotion to Wittenberg and for his honesty of purpose that he should have so readily protected Luther in the very difficult years through which he was soon to pass. He neither then nor later seems to have displayed very much spiritual perception. He had augmented the reputation of the collegiate church by compiling an extraordinarily capricious collection of relics. Andreas Meinhard's official catalogue, drawn up in 1509, listed 5,005 items, including 204 pieces associated with the innocent children slain by Herod; one historian has estimated that the 17,000 articles on display in 1518 carried with them possible indulgences of 127,799 years and 116 days. The Elector's object in making the collection may have been similar to that which led him to found the university, to foster the fame of Wittenberg and to attract pilgrims to its church. If he had been graced with deeper spiritual insight, he might well have hesitated before giving his support to the man who so effectively challenged the whole notion of indulgences. Luther's patron was a capable, honest fellow who resented dictation, whether

4   Luther's Father
*From a portrait by Lucas Cranach
the Elder, c. 1527*

5   Luther's Mother
*From a portrait by Lucas Cranach
the Elder, c. 1527*

6 Martin Luther
From a portrait by Lucas Cranach the Elder

it came from the Pope or the Emperor. In general he had his eye to the main chance, but in an age of Machiavellian diplomacy he had more conscience than many of his contemporaries.

Luther can have had no conception of what the future had in store when he went to Wittenberg, first as junior lecturer in 1508–9, and later as a full professor. Although he was not by any means free from administrative and pastoral responsibilities, his main task was academic. The faculty numbered some men of real distinction, among them Andreas Carlstadt who was at this time the chief exponent of the older school of theology, the Thomists or Realists, Nikolaus von Amsdorf who held to the Scotist tradition in his studies and Trutvetter, the principal representative of the nominalist school, who returned to Erfurt in 1510. Luther's closest intimate was the Saxon Vicar-General of his order, John Staupitz, who held the Chair of Biblical Theology. Twenty years older than Luther, attractive, sincere, scholarly, Staupitz had played a leading part in supporting the friars who strove for a return to the original austerity of their rule. He was well versed in scholastic theology, in all probability more of a Thomist than his friend, and genuinely concerned with the interior spiritual life. Staupitz realised that religion did not consist in ceremonial or rule but in bringing a man to God. He was well equipped to advise Luther in the doubts and difficulties that were soon to assail him. He perceived too his academic promise and to that end in 1512 persuaded Luther to take his doctorate in theology, the fees for which were paid by the Elector at Staupitz's request, in order that he might exchange his Chair of Moral Philosophy for that of Biblical Theology which Staupitz now held.

For the next five years Luther was mainly but not exclusively concerned with the study of theology. He acquired an extraordinarily thorough knowledge of the Scriptures and a good command over the conventional equipment for glossing and interpreting them, reading the ponderous, erudite commentaries of the great medieval scholars. Much of his time was spent in instructing his pupils through the medium of lectures. Using the text of the Bible as the foundation, Luther construed the book which he was studying chapter by chapter, verse by verse, employing a gloss or commentary compiled from the set authors to elucidate the meaning, and adding, where necessary, his own comments. The medieval theologian inherited a corpus of material, involving often over-elaborate and sophisticated methods of interpretation which submerged the literal meaning in a flood of allegory. The chief text was still the *Sentences* of the twelfth-century

dis heiligthumbs

Zum .xj. ein kleyn silberē vnubergult Monstrantz

Von Sant Cecilia
xix . partickel

Zum .xij. Ein Berlin mutter mit silber vberguldt oben ein lawen

Von sant Felicola ein partickel
Von sant Fidentia ein partickel
Von sant Eugenia ein partickel
Von sant Gasilla ein partickel
Vom gebein sant Anastasie .xxij. partick.
Ein zahn von sant. Anastasia
Vom gebein sant Agathe .iiij. partickel
Von dem gebein sant Apolonie . vij. ptic.
Von einem zahn sant Apolonie .j. ptickel
Zwen Zehn von sant Apolonia
Von dem Sarck sant Agnetis ein partic.
Jungkfraw vnd merterin
Vom Klaydt Agnetis ein partic.   Von yrem heiligen gebein .xv. pti.
Ein zahn sant Agnetis   Von yrem hirnschedel ein partickel
Von yrem heiligen haupt ein ptic.   Vom gebein sant Lucie. vij. ptic.
Ein Zahn von sant Lucia   Suma .lxjx. ptickel   B ij

7   Relics (from a contemporary catalogue)
at the Castle Church, Wittenberg

theologian, Peter Lombard, for whose work even in later life Luther expressed his admiration. Biblical commentary had thus been erected into an imposing but ultimately unrealistic superstructure of systematic theology. Lecture courses on biblical books could last for years; Henry of Langenstein, it was said, had taken 13 years to cover three or four chapters. Under the guidance of a prosaic lecturer this form of instruction was capable of becoming intolerably arid, but a genuine scholar could make it a rich intellectual experience.

The defects of the approach now seem obvious. It crushed intellectual initiative, barring any approach which did not fall within the accepted framework of study. In the later Middle Ages it had tended to become ever increasingly elaborate. If it could be intellectually titivating, it bore little obvious relation to the practical realities of existence or to the problems of spiritual life. It was basically conservative and pedagogic. The emergence of nominalism had in practice only led to the familiar stock-in-trade of the scholastic theologian being placed in a different juxtaposition. It had already earned the intense contempt of Erasmus and other humanists, and it was soon to merit the not wholly deserved execration of Luther himself.

His first years at Wittenberg, however, gave no real hint of the future, though he was already moving quietly outside the traditional syllabus. He began the study of Greek and Hebrew to understand better the original text. He started a thorough study of the works of the great African father, St. Augustine. This was to constitute a landmark in his theological development, so that by 1516 he could describe the chief ingredients in his work as the Bible, St. Augustine and the Fathers. As early as 1509 he had written to John Braun, declaring that he would readily exchange the study of theology for that of the philosophy in which he was then engaged, 'that theology which extracts the nut from the shell, the grain from the husk, the marrow from the bone'; and the marginal notes which he prepared on the *Sentences* of Lombard include some denigratory comments on Aristotle and the study of philosophy.

Indeed in theological controversy he was already assertive and self-possessed. When the humanist, Jakob Wimpheling, criticised his order, Luther dismissed him as an 'aged and distracted scarecrow'. Yet he was necessarily saturated in contemporary theology. His reasoning powers had been shaped by a training in systematic logic. He had become familiar with the different shades of meaning borne by theological concepts such as grace. Under nominalist influence he was able to distinguish between works which were enacted before an infusion of divine grace and those which had been done after it. Aware that God's will was completely sovereign and unfettered, he must equally have seen man as inclined to sin and saved by faith.

Moreover, his mind was beginning to be torn by inner tensions which the religious life had not happily solved. He was to an increasing extent aware of the wrath of God and his inability either to escape from it or to allay it. 'Who knows', he asked himself after a round of exhausting services and mortifications, 'whether these things please God?' 'The more I sweated it out like this, the less peace and quiet I experienced.' The more he searched the Scriptures, the more puzzled he became. He seemed the victim of a spiritual conflict which was incapable of solution. 'It is', he wrote later, 'God's eternity, holiness and power which thus continuously threaten man throughout the whole of his life. . . . God's ever-present judgment clutches man in the loneliness of his conscience, and with his every breath conveys him to the Almighty and Holy One to prosper or destroy.' In his isolation he was confronted by God, but as yet he fought against necessary dependence upon His righteousness. And then, in the lamp-lit cell his readings in St. Paul and St. Augustine, illuminated by mystical theology, began to open new and ultimately dramatic vistas.

CHAPTER 3

The Young Professor and the Beginnings of the Break with Rome

1512–1518

Luther's last years as an Augustinian friar were a most vital period in the evolution of his theology and of his religious position. From 1512 to 1513 Luther, spiritually uneasy, moved theologically away from orthodox teaching. At first his thinking took place within the schemata of the medieval schoolmen, and his methodology was the familiar merchandise of the professional theologians of his age, text, gloss or comment and scholia or essay; but the Sacred Scriptures in which his mind became so saturated formed the central feature of his study.

The course of lectures which he gave on the Psalms in 1513–14 made him the more aware of the richness of St. Augustine's thought and by the time he had concluded his discourses there was more than a hint that the discovery of Augustine was associated with a growing repugnancy for Aristotle. The African saint had an emotional depth and an interior spirituality which threw into relief the aridity of Aristotle. 'Instead of Christ and Paul we were accustomed to learn Averroes and Aristotle in the schools', he declared later, alleging that the schoolmen were to blame for tying the interpretation of God's Word to Aristotelian philosophy. Throughout his life the Psalter was to be for Luther an invaluable commentary on Christian life. 'Would you see the Holy Christian Church portrayed with living colour and form, fastened together in one place, take your Psalter, and you have a fine, crystal-clear mirror which will show you what Christianity is.' In his lectures Luther still employed the fourfold exegesis familiar to medieval scholars; the Psalms were not to be taken literally but as foreshadowing Christ, allegorising the Church, teaching right conduct to the individual soul and referring to the end of all things. Yet it seems probable that Luther came to a fresh perception of the meaning of God's justice during these lectures; 'the Justice of God', he wrote of Psalm 70, 'is all this: to abase oneself to the uttermost and this properly Christ expresses here'.

In the autumn of 1515, Luther began a new course of lectures on St. Paul's *Epistle to the Romans*, lasting from November 3rd, 1515 to September 7th, 1516. He prepared these with great care. Helped by the edition of the Pauline Epistles published by the French humanist, Lefèvre (whose commentary on the Psalms he had already used for his previous course), and by his study of St. Augustine (from whose works there were at least some 120 quotations), he went very thoroughly into the meaning of the text. Before he had completed his work Luther was able to make use of the new edition of the New Testament prepared by Erasmus. That he did so so quickly after its appearance shows that he was receptive to new ideas. Luther was never a humanist but he was ready to utilise the tools they had created. Biblical humanism laid its impress on nominalist philosophy. His study of the Greek New Testament led to the steady abandonment of the medieval method of exegesis and to a concern with the literal truth of the text, the *sensus literalis, grammaticus, historicus*. He was anxious to interpret the text accurately, readily abandoning an exposition which was grammatically untenable; 'in translating I always keep this rule; we must not contend against grammar'. He insisted on a good knowledge of the original language in which the Bible was written and very readily used all the lexicons, commentaries and critical editions which could help in elucidating the sacred text. Yet interpretation and elucidation were ultimately dependent upon his own religious experience and the apprehension of fundamental doctrinal truths to which, as he believed, this had given rise. 'Languages', he was to write later, 'do not make a theologian: they are only a help. Before a man can speak on anything, he must first know and understand his subject.'

This was not indeed plain when he started to lecture on the *Epistle to the Romans*. Even so, he appeared more concerned than he had been in his previous course to approach the text literally and directly. The text of the Epistle reinforced the emphasis on the will of God which he had learned from his nominalist teachers. By contrast man as a sinner is hopelessly ill-equipped to win God's favour to work out his own salvation. 'The sum and substance of this Epistle', he tells his pupils, 'is to disperse and eliminate all the righteousness and wisdom of the flesh and on the other hand to confirm, increase, and magnify sin and nothingness, so that finally Christ and his righteousness may enter into us in place of those things which are wiped out. For in God's presence man does not become just by doing just works, but by being just, he does just deeds.' The impotence of the human will to procure man's salvation ran like a thread through his exposition. 'Why does man take pride in his merit and his works, which in no way please because they have merit or are good, but because they have been chosen by God from eternity that they should please Him? Therefore we have no good works except the search for grace, because our works do not make us good, but our goodness, or rather the goodness of God, makes us and our works good.' The sinner will not be saved by his own exertions but by grace conferred from without. 'For God wills to save us, not by a righteousness and wisdom from within but from without. Not that which comes and is born from ourselves. But that which comes from without into us. Not that which rises from the earth, but that which comes down from heaven.' 'Just is a man reckoned so to be by God, but because he is reckoned to be just by God, therefore he is just.' But he stressed, as he continued to do throughout the remainder of his life, that faith is much more than mere intellectual assent. It is an active quality which enables us to commune with God and to serve him. 'Always', as he wrote, 'a sinner, always a penitent, always right with God.' His lectures showed that he had begun to shed the nominalist belief that God will infuse his grace into those who try their best. The humbled will is the only road to grace. 'In our ignorance justified', he wrote, 'in our knowledge unjustified; sinners in fact, but righteous in hope.'

In contrast to this harsh if realistic view of man there was the abundant promise not merely of faith but of what had already been accomplished by Christ on man's behalf, of which the Epistle speaks. 'It is a mistake to believe that this evil is remedied by works, since experience proves that in spite of all our good works the desire for evil persists and that no one is free from it, not even a day-old child. But God's mercy is such that, although this evil endures, it is not reckoned as sin for those who call upon Him and with signs beseech Him to deliver them. . . . Thus we are sinners and yet we are accounted righteous by God through faith.' The course of lectures makes plain the direction in which Luther's mind was working. Nourished by Augustinian and Pauline thought, he had become critical of the ideas which he had once firmly accepted. He sees that the human will is powerless to secure man's salvation and that God alone can save by His grace. He believed already that faith ultimately justifies the sinner, though he had not yet realised the full implications of this belief. In other words, he was beginning in this respect also to discard the nominalist ideas which had done so much to condition his thought. Occam had taught that God ensures that a man could be saved without sanctifying grace or works of merit because God's will was total, *a sola divina acceptatione*. God was able to infuse His own righteousness into man so that his own sinful nature no longer counted as a barrier to his acceptance by God. Luther had held such views but he had now grown out of them. God could accept man without works of merit or sanctifying grace because Christ had already by His own atonement made this possible. Occam's hypothesis that God can save us if we will by His arbitrary decrees has been turned by Luther into the declaration that God has saved us arbitrarily by the work of Christ and through our faith in His promises. He may have originally approached the *Epistle to the Romans* from the standpoint of a nominalist philosopher but he had reached very different conclusions.

It was natural that he should turn from the *Epistle to the Romans* to the *Epistle to the Galatians* with which it is so closely allied, and upon which in 1531 he was to write one of his most penetrating and important commentaries. The lectures were prepared quickly and were delivered between October 27th, 1516 and March 3rd, 1517. A young Augustinian friar from Cologne, Augustine Himmel, who attended them has left a portrait of the lecturer. 'He was a man of middling height, with a voice both sharp and gentle: it was soft in

8 Pope Leo X
*From a crayon drawing
variously attributed to
Sebastiano del Piombo
and Giulio Romano*

9 Pope Clement VII
*From a portrait by
Sebastiano del Piombo*

10   Frederick the Wise, Elector of Saxony
From a portrait by Albrecht Dürer, c. 1496

tone, sharp in the enunciation of syllables, words and sentences. He spoke neither too rapidly nor too slowly, but evenly and without hesitation, as well as very clearly, and so logically that each part flowed naturally out of what went before. He did not get lost in a maze of language, but first expounded the individual words, then the sentences, so that one could see how the content of the exposition arose, and flowed out of the text itself. For it all hung together in order, word, matter, natural and moral philosophy . . . there was never anything in his lectures that was not relevant and full of meaning.' Luther again made considerable use of Erasmus' Greek Testament and expressed his indebtedness to St. Jerome, declaring in his marginalia that 'in this whole Epistle Jerome pleases me more than Augustine'. Yet, in fact, Augustine's influence was still paramount, more especially in the renewed emphasis which he placed on justification by faith. In his lectures he was necessarily concerned with developing the dialectic between the Law and the Gospel. 'The Law is the Word of Moses to us, the Gospel, on the other hand, is the Word of God in us.' 'For the Law and the Righteousness of the Law are the shadow and figure of the Gospel, and of the righteousness of faith.' 'Faith', he urged, 'abolishes sin, wrath and death, because it justifies, brings peace and makes alive in Christ who is made to us righteousness, peace and life.'

He turned in March, 1517, from the *Epistle to the Galatians* to the *Epistle to the Hebrews*, the Pauline authorship of which he queried though its teaching fitted in well with his own presuppositions. He lectured twice a week from 6.0 to 7.0 in the morning, and sometimes from 12.0 to 1.0 in the afternoon as well. These lectures, in which he made much use of the Homilies of St. Chrysostom on the Epistle, displayed his growing linguistic facility and his capacity to make use of humanistic scriptural texts. The theme of the Epistle bore some relation to his own spiritual struggles. It proclaimed the triumph of the Cross over the Devil and all his works. 'For in such a way God advances His own purpose and fulfils it through His 'strange work', with marvellous wisdom, compelling the Devil by means of death to forward nothing except life, and so when it appears to operate most in opposition to God's purpose, it actually works with his 'own work' for God.' 'O it is a wonderful thing', he said in his lectures, 'to be a Christian man, and have a hidden life, not secreted in some cell, with the hermits, or even in the human heart, which is an unfathomable abyss, but in the invisible God Himself, and so to live within the world and yet to feed on Him who never appears except through the hearing of the Word.'

His biblical studies had really opened a new world, different from and indeed hostile to that in which he had been intellectually cradled. In the autumn of 1516 a public disputation was held at Wittenberg in which he opposed the nominalist teaching on grace. About the same time he declared that 'Our theology and St. Augustine are going ahead, and reign in our University, and it is God's work. Aristotle is gradually declining, perhaps into everlasting perdition. It is marvellous how the lectures on the *Sentences* are no longer in favour. Nobody can hope for an audience unless he professes this theology, i.e. the Bible or St. Augustine, or some doctor of real authority in the Church.' Clearly the Word of God was already assuming for Luther the status of a basic authority. In his exposition of the Seven Penitential Psalms in 1517 he abandoned the fourfold method of exegesis and in his interpretation of the Decalogue in 1518 he criticised the schoolmen who 'play with' the meaning of the scriptural text as though it was a game. 'When I was a monk', he wrote later somewhat unjustly, 'they used to scorn the Bible. Nobody understood the Psalter. They used to believe that the *Epistle to the Romans* contained some controversies about the matters of Paul's day and was irrelevant to our age. Scotus, Thomas, Aristotle were the books to read.'

This was, however, not the only interesting thing about the lectures that he was delivering during these years. There were here and there clear indications that he was concerned with the abuses within the Church, and with the low standards prevailing among the clergy: 'those foolish and impious churchmen who swagger about with the gifts which they have received from the laity and think they are doing their job when they mutter a few prayers on behalf of their benefactors'. 'One is amazed', he declared, 'at the thick darkness of our time. Spiritual persons, those devourers of temporalities on a grand scale, indeed bear nothing with greater impatience than any defiance of the liberties, rights and powers of the Church; when this occurs they quickly let loose all the lightnings of excommunication, proclaim the offenders heretics and brand them with astounding audacity as enemies of God, the Church and the Apostles Peter and Paul. . . . Thus they proclaim that obedience and faith consist in preserving, extending and defending temporal things.' Such criticisms, biting though they might be, were literary commonplaces at the time and far paler than the satirical writing of a Brandt or an Erasmus. They show, however, that Luther was becoming steadily more and more aware of the contrast between what he held to be the life of the primitive Church and that of his own day.

His outlook was affected, though to a less extent than has sometimes been claimed, by his reading of mystical theology. The educated laity as well as many of the clergy found in the writings of the mystics a devotional guide to help them to come into that unity with God which the hastily-muttered offices of the Church and the aridities of contemporary scholasticism could not provide. Luther himself read some of the writings of St. Bernard of Clairvaux, St. Bonaventure and Gerson. His friend, the Augustinian Vicar-General, very probably drew his attention to the sermons of the fifteenth-century German mystic, John Tauler, who had resolved his own spiritual tensions by a passive acceptance of the divine will. 'For the reception of the first grace as well as of the full glory, we must hold ourselves ever passive like a woman at conception. For we are the bride of Christ; so before grace comes we should pray and implore, but when it comes and the soul is penetrated by the spirit we ought neither to pray nor exert ourselves, but only to remain passive. This is, in truth, difficult, and causes violent affliction, for when the spirit surrenders all understanding and desire, it takes flight into the shadows and, as it were, passes into perdition and destruction. Then the soul seeks with all its power to escape and so it often happens that it is robbed of the finest gifts.' But Tauler also believed that such acceptance of the divine will must lead to good works. 'Life does not consist in repose, but in progress from good to better.' About the same time, probably in 1516, Luther read and became enthusiastic about another mystical work, the *Theologica Germanica*. Such mystical writings helped to confirm the conclusions which he was beginning to formulate about the inward nature of religion.

Personally he was in a state of spiritual strain. He had been most conscientious in seeking to carry out the rules of his order, so much so that his friends warned him against the dangers to his health that this involved. 'When I was a monk I tried most assiduously to live according to the Rule, and I used to be contrite, to confess and enumerate my sins, and I frequently repeated my confession, and diligently performed my allotted penance' and yet he only emerged 'uncertain, weaker, more troubled.' He began to wonder whether his efforts were really pleasing to God. 'Ah!' his friends would say to him, 'What are you so anxious about? It isn't necessary. Just be humble and patient. Do you think God requires such strictness from you? He knows what you are thinking, and He is good.' But Luther remembered that God was just as well as good, and that as a sinner he stood within the shadow of His wrath. 'In the monastery, I did not think about women, or gold, or goods, but my heart trembled, and I doubted how God could be gracious to me. Then I fell away from faith, and let myself think nothing less than that I can come under the wrath of God, whom I must propitiate with my good works.' But works, he saw more and more clearly, would not avail to save him from the possibility of eternal damnation. In 1518 he wrote: 'Then God appears dreadfully angry and with him, the whole of his creation. There is no possibility of escape or relief, either within or without but all is accusation. . . . At this moment . . . the soul cannot believe that it can ever be consoled . . . [it] is . . . left only with the naked longing for help, and terrifying fearfulness, but it does not know whence aid can come. This represents the soul stretched out with Christ, so that all a man's bones can be numbered, nor is there any niche that is not filled with the most bitter pain, horror, fear, and grief . . .'

His despair was so profound that it affected his health. He would wake in a cold sweat. He suffered much from constipation. The Devil and his agents were an unwholesome and ever-present reality. He felt tempted by what he described as *concupiscentia*, not indeed to be interpreted as sexual lust, but as self-love or egocentricity. He was too much 'turned in upon himself'. Possibly too the attempt to wear down the flesh did create the conditions for a lively imagination to work upon the temptations which the call to chastity and poverty reinforced. His involvement in teaching and administration did not provide an adequate outlet for his energies. He was tortured not merely by a sense of insufficiency but of impotence to win God's forgiveness. 'I myself', he wrote in 1525, 'have more than once been offended [by the doctrine of predestination] almost to the very depth and abyss of despair, so that I wished I had never been created a man, until I realised how salutary was this despair, and how near to grace.'

So mind and body, character and personality, helped not merely in the formation of the ideas which his rejection of Aristotelian scholasticism produced, but fostered a religious experience which led inevitably to a form of spiritualc risis. His sensitivity and scrupulosity caused an almost obsessive concern with his own sinful nature. The Church's machinery of penitence was totally inadequate to reassure him. It is impossible to treat of single sins, he urged, when the whole nature of man is corrupt. No man can make satisfactory amends to God for his sin. Indeed no man can effectively know when he is really and truly contrite. His friend and faithful adviser, Staupitz, did what he could to hearten him, stressing the work of grace which Christ can perform in the human soul. 'There is', he told Brother Martin, 'no true penitence which does not begin with a love of righteousness and of God, and this love which others think to be the end of penitence is rather its beginning.'

Luther found the answer to his spiritual anxiety in the doctrine of justification by faith which was to sustain him throughout the remainder of his life. In spite of all that he had done to try to win God's favour, he had not experienced the peace of mind which he believed that acceptance by God should bring. Good works had proved to be of no avail. He was living in a state of spiritual tension, ever more and more aware of his own impotence and of God's wrath, displayed through plague, famine and violence, and ultimately in the punishment of hell. 'For in this existence God punishes the impious to terrify the rest of the ungodly and to show them that they too will not go unpunished.' But, he, Luther was also one of the ungodly. What hope had he of mercy? He experienced the inexpressible possibility of eternal damnation. 'The soul deprived of all confidence is placed in a horrifying condition as a guilty criminal, standing alone before the tribunal of an eternal and angry God . . . the conscience being sentenced and convicted immediately senses nothing but that eternal damnation which is its lot; nobody can comprehend this profound experience nor indeed its secondary manifestations unless he has tasted it: and therefore we cannot fully describe it when dealing with it. Job experienced it more than any other.' 'In addition to being alarmed and terrified by God's wrath, man can find consolation in no creature and whatever he looks at appears opposed to him. For the whole creation acts with its creator: and especially when a man's conscience is against God; and as a result everything appears angry; everything adds to his wretchedness: all things around are enemies.' 'In this state, hope despairs and despair hopes; and nothing seems alive but that inward groaning that cannot be uttered in which the Spirit ascends, moving upon the face of these waters veiled in darkness . . . no one can understand these things but he who has tasted them. . . .' This had indeed been Luther's own experience. 'For, however virtuously I lived as a monk, in God's presence I felt that I was a sinner with a most uneasy conscience nor had I any confidence that I had pleased him with my satisfaction', he wrote towards the end of his life. 'I did not love, nay, rather I hated this just God who punished sinners and if not with "open blasphemy" certainly with excessive murmuring I was angry with God.' What could save him from the pit of despair?

Confronted with such a challenge, he became increasingly fascinated by the meaning of God's justice. It appeared less and less as the strict, retributive justice which he had once thought that it was, but as a gift of God made available for all his children. 'The just', as the famous phrase from the *Epistle to the Romans*, i, 17, put it, 'shall live by faith'. 'At last, God being merciful, as I meditated day and night on the interconnection of the words, namely, "the Justice of God is revealed in it, as it is written, 'the Just shall live by Faith'," there I began to comprehend the Justice of God as that by which the just lives by the gift of God, namely by faith, and this sentence, "the Justice of God is revealed in the gospel", to be that passive justice, with which the merciful God justifies us, by faith, as it is written, "The just lives by faith". This straightway made me feel as though reborn, and as though I had entered through open gates into paradise itself. From then on, the whole face of scripture appeared different.' 'Because he trembled before God's punishing Justice', it has been stated,[1] 'felt himself crushed by it, and yet recognised its verdict honestly as true, he was enabled to apprehend its final meaning. God does not send his Grace alongside his justice . . . but he sends it through his justice. . . . God is nothing but sheer goodness, which is always giving itself.' 'I knew Christ', he wrote, 'as none other than a strict judge, from whose face I wanted to flee, and yet could not'; but he had come to a new apprehension of what God's justice should mean to the believer. If God's justice is interpreted in too pedantic a fashion, then all man-kind must be irretrievably damned since every man is, and remains, a sinner in God's sight. Luther was continuously, scrupulously conscious of the gravity, permeability and ubiquity of sin, that *amor sui*, the inner egoism which endlessly battles for the control of man's soul.

But because God is merciful, loving and just, He wills to save the sinner. Christ makes this possible through his sacrifice on the Cross. 'He [i.e. St. Paul] speaks against those arrogant people who believe they can come to God apart from Christ, as though it was enough for them to have believed, and thus *sola fide* not through Christ but beside Christ or beyond Christ, not needing him having once accepted the grace of justification . . . but it is necessary to have Christ always, heretofore and to eternity as mediator of such faith . . . it must be "through faith" "through Christ" so that all that we do or are able to suffer may be through faith in Christ, and yet in all these things we acknowledge ourselves to be unprofitable servants, and by Christ alone, do we consider ourselves able to have access to God. For so it is

[1] Quoted from Gordon Rupp, *The Righteousness of God* (1953), 127; to which I am much indebted in this chapter..

in all the works of faith, that we are made worthy in the refuge and protection of Christ and His righteousness.' 'Therefore we are justified by faith' and our sins are remitted 'but it is through Jesus Christ our Lord.' 'This', he said in a sermon, 'is the nature of faith that it boldly takes the grace of God for granted, forms an opinion of confidence towards Him, and feels assured that God will regard him favourably and not forsake him. . . . Faith does not require information, knowledge or certainty, but free submission and joyful venturing upon God's unfelt, untried and unrecognised goodness.'

Man has to throw himself completely on God's mercy in order that he may discover the immensity of the divine forgiveness. In one place Luther compares God with a master craftsman. He reveals the poverty of his apprentices' work by placing their work beside his own. Then by demonstrating his own work he imparts his skill to his workmen. 'And so the just God makes us worthy of credit, because he makes us like Himself.' Man, aware of the depth of his sin, humbly prostrates himself before God and justified through Christ is released from bondage to sin. All that God requires of him is faith. 'For without faith it is impossible for God to work or to be with us, as he himself never does anything without his Word. Therefore none can co-operate with him, unless he abides by the Word, which he can only do through faith, as an instrument cannot co-operate with the craftsman unless it is grasped in his hand.' Man remains a sinner but is yet justified by faith in the sight of God. *Semper peccator, semper justus.* 'God wants sinners only. . . . God has nothing to do with holy men' because a holy man is a self-contradiction. God accepts 'believing sinners' rather than 'sanctified saints'. 'Christ was given', he was to write in his *Commentary on the Galatians* at a later date, 'not for pretended or fictitious sins, but for real ones; not for little sins, but for huge ones; not for this sin or that sin, but for all sins . . .' This is God's doing alone. 'Not by our merits, but by sheer election and his immutable will . . . by his undeviating love are we saved. And thus he proves through all these things, not our will, but his inflexible and sure will of predestination.' Yet if faith alone justifies, it cannot justify without creating the good works which form its inevitable corollary. If the Christian is guided by the Holy Spirit and is aware of Christ's presence at work within himself by faith his life must undergo a re-orientation. 'Wherever the works of Christ are absent, there Christ, too, is absent.' 'It is faith in Christ which makes him live in me and move in me and act in me: in the same way as a healing ointment acts on a sick body and we are hereby not only made one flesh and one body with Christ;

but have an intimate, ineffable exchange of our sins for his righteousness, as the venerable sacrament of the altar shows us, where bread
and wine are transformed into the body and blood of Christ.' 'When
a man believes God, whether he fasts, or prays or serves a brother, is
all one and the same: for he knows that he serves and pleases God
equally whether his works be great or small, precious or vile, short or
long.' 'Works and ceremonies are performed in faith and love, where
they are not done from any constraining necessity, nor because they
are commanded, but when they are done in the freedom of spirit.'
'Faith receives Christ's good works; love performs good works for the
neighbours.'

Luther only realised slowly the full implications of what the doctrine
of justification by faith meant for him and for the Church; but he had at
least become convinced of its ultimate necessity before the quarrel with
the Papacy opened. It is said that he first became fully aware of the
meaning of the phrase from Romans when he was sitting on the stool,
secretus locus monachorum, or *cloaca*, in the tower room of the monastery at Wittenberg in 1514; though it is at least possible that the room
was *hypocaustum*, simply the monastic calefactory or warming room.
It is, however, fair to stress that Luther's personal experience was a
strong blend of mind, body and soul. Throughout life too he suffered
much from constipation as from an anxiety; in such circumstances a
successful evacuation could be a physical and almost a spiritual
liberation. Whatever the interpretation to be placed upon this
Turmerlebnis or tower experience, there can be no doubt that Luther's
mental and spiritual tensions had their counterpart in a measure of
physical infirmity, and that his theology was rooted not merely in the
working of a powerful mind and in his spiritual development, but in
the totality of his experience.

It is against this setting that the question of indulgences which
brought him into the public eye for the first time must be set. Indulgences were a by-product of the medieval stratagem of penance, with
its threefold requirements of contrition, confession and satisfaction.
The Church, so it was taught, through the existence of a treasury of
merit, accrued by the infinite merits of Christ and the saints, had the
right to distribute the benefit of these merits in consideration of the
prayers or pious works undertaken by the faithful. Plenary indulgences,
that is a remission of all temporal punishment due to sin, had been
promised in the twelfth century to those who went on crusade. An
indulgence implied therefore the commutation of the act of satisfaction,
but it did not eliminate the need either of contrition or confession. In

1300 Pope Boniface VIII had inaugurated a jubilee indulgence for all the faithful who visited the tomb of the Apostles at Rome on 15 successive days. The indulgence was discovered to be a remunerative financial transaction and was repeated at increasingly regular intervals. In 1476 Pope Sixtus IV declared that souls in purgatory were able to benefit through the medium of an indulgence:

> *Sobald das Geld in Kasten klingt*
> *Die Seele aus dem Fegefeuer springt.*

Whatever the theological safeguards against the abuse of the system of indulgences, the laity came to believe that the payment of money could bring about a remission of penalty in the afterlife. On All Saints' Day, 1516, Luther had preached on the question of indulgences in the Castle Church at Wittenberg, a topical issue in such surroundings where the collection of relics carried indulgences for those who visited them. In February, 1517, he made a more penetrating attack on what seemed to him to be a peculiarly unpleasing way of lulling the sinner to a sense of false security.

The problem of indulgences had been brought to his notice through the activities of a Dominican friar, John Tetzel, who was acting as an agent for the Archbishop of Mainz. The Archbishop, Albert of Brandenburg, a splendid young man of humanist leanings, who was already Archbishop of Magdeburg and administrator of the see of Halberstadt, had wished to add to his ecclesiastical dignities through the acquisition of the Archbishopric of Mainz which carried with it the right to elect the Holy Roman Emperor. The fees involved in his promotion were more than he could pay in cash: 21,000 ducats for the pallium alone and 10,000 ducats for the papal dispensation which permitted him to hold his sees in plurality. He borrowed money from the south German banking house of Fugger, but he was faced with the difficult problem of repayment. Someone had the bright idea of utilising the indulgence system. The proceeds were to be divided between the Pope to help in the building of the new St. Peter's at Rome and the Fuggers to liquidate the Archbishop's debt. The scheme doubtless seemed to its sponsors shrewd, sensible and unobjectionable. The faithful would be urged to genuine penitence and contrition as well as enjoined to contribute to the reconstruction of the shrine which housed the relics of the blessed Apostle, St. Peter. The papal bull authorising the indulgences made it plain that absolution depended upon genuine repentance and confession, albeit other phrases might have suggested another interpretation. The indulgence promised four privileges, a

61

11   The sale of indulgences
From Bainton, 'Here I Stand', Abingdon Press

plenary remission of all sins, the choice of a confessor by the penitent, participation in the merits of the saints and the release of souls in purgatory. People have often contributed to less worthy charities, but for the most part they took a simple view of what was offered to them. Tetzel himself had the makings of a first-class salesman. He had special sermons printed and his arrival was heralded with excellent publicity and colourful ceremonial. He had not indeed been permitted to enter the Electorate of Saxony, where he might have seemed to be impinging upon the Elector's own monopoly in these matters; if any Saxon wished to buy an indulgence he had only to visit the Castle Church at Wittenberg.

Luther in his then state of mind was, however, appalled by what he learned not merely of Tetzel's energy and success but by the way in which the Wittenbergers themselves crossed the Saxon frontier to avail themselves of the spiritual bargains which the Dominican friar was handing out. In October, 1517, on the eve of All Saints' Day, he gave notice on the door of the Castle Church that he would defend in academic disputation 95 theses criticising indulgences. His action was well timed, since it was the eve of the patronal festival when the

Elector's huge collection was visited by the faithful who earned indulgence by so doing. It was his deliberate intention to prove that the doctrine of indulgences contravened the teaching of the Gospel. He cannot at this moment have foreseen that what he was doing was necessarily heterodox. Indeed he sent copies of the theses to the Archbishop of Mainz and his ecclesiastical superior, the Bishop of Brandenburg. It was a quarter of a century later that he wrote: 'I was completely dead to the world until God deemed that the time had come; then Junker Tetzel excited me with indulgences and Dr. Staupitz spurred me on against the Pope.' But in fact Luther had in November, 1517, very little idea of where his criticisms were likely to lead him.

What was the content of these theses? He repeated that while Christ required the sinner to repent, the change wrought by such repentance is very different from the punishment which the Church demands of the sinner. 'When our Lord and Master, Jesus Christ, said, *Poenitentiam Agite* . . . he wished the entire life of believers to be one of penitence.' He attacked the behaviour of indulgence sellers who deceived the people as to the true nature of an indulgence. The Pope cannot possibly have any power over souls in purgatory. 'Christians', he concluded, 'should be exhorted that they study to follow Christ, their head, through the pains of death and hell, and let them rather hope to enter heaven through much tribulation than to confide in the security of peace.' Luther, the modern German writer, Bonhoeffer, has phrased it, had opposed the doctrine of 'costly grace' to that of 'cheap grace'. For the rest the theses accepted the full authority of the Pope and the existence of purgatory.

Why did these theses create such an uproar? They received unusual publicity. Within a fortnight they had been printed and were circulating throughout Germany. Luther had the support of his fellow professors as well as of the Elector who seems to have been more concerned with the academic renown that Luther was winning for his university than with the implied criticism of his own collection of relics. On the other hand, Luther's blatant attack on Tetzel had greatly irritated his fellow Dominicans who drew up their own series of theses and early in 1518 charged Luther with heresy at Rome. Similarly, the Archbishop of Mainz instructed the theologians and jurists of his local university to report on Luther's statements, and to despatch a copy to Rome. By referring the matter directly to the Pope the Archbishop avoided a head-on conflict with the Elector of Saxony and the Augustinian Order. Neither the Dominicans nor the Archbishop can have had any idea about the capacity, courage or obstinacy of their opponent.

Nor for that matter could the Roman authorities have had the least notion as to what the future held in store. It was only on February 3rd, 1518, that Pope Leo X, the polished dilettante who then occupied the papal throne, ordered the recently-elected Augustinian general, Gabriel Venetus, to bring his recalcitrant inferior to heel. This was easier said than done. Although Luther sincerely believed that his cause was right, he was clearly enjoying the limelight. He could not disguise from himself that as a result of his stand he had created a following among the professors and students; the Saxon court chaplain and librarian, Spalatin, represented his cause with the Elector himself. He could not be as easily 'soothed' or 'quietened' as the Romans hoped.

The printing press undoubtedly helped to harden Luther's opinions. The sermon on indulgences which he published in the spring of 1518 to the consternation of Bishop Schulze of Brandenburg was a more outspoken condemnation of indulgences than the theses had been. 'It is my desire and . . . advice that no one shall buy indulgences. Let indolent and sleepy Christians purchase them and go your own way.' He declared trenchantly that it is impossible to remit the pains of purgatory through the purchase of indulgences. He dismissed his critics with typical contempt: 'a few morons who never smelled the Bible or read a word of Christian doctrine'. After the Easter festival of 1518, protected by a safe-conduct from the Elector, Luther left Wittenberg to attend the triennial meeting of the Augustinian chapters at Heidelberg. One of his followers, Leonard Beyer, aroused the anger of the conservative faction by attacking scholastic teaching and by asserting the doctrine of justification by faith, but one of those present, the redoubtable future scholar, Martin Bucer, was won over to Luther at Heidelberg. 'As Christ turned to the heathen when the Jews rejected Him, so now let His true theology which these deluded old men reject, be presented to the young.' It was perhaps a portent that Luther's strongest support came from the younger friars and students, who were ready to reject the old tried ways for more exciting intellectual fashions.

Luther himself was now at work on a strongly-worded apologia which he intended to address to the Pope himself. He asked Staupitz if he would ensure its despatch, stressing his own debt to his old friend and ending on a note which was a typical compound of humility and pride: 'As for the rest I have nothing further to add to my threatening friends except a remark of Reuchlin's: "Whoever is poor fears nothing, for he can lose nothing". Possessions I neither have nor want

. . . only one thing is left to me, my poor weak body, exhausted by incessant hardship. If they destroy it through violence or guile . . . perhaps they will make me poorer by one or two hours of life. My sweet Redeemer and Mediator, Jesus Christ, whom I will praise my life long, is all-sufficient for me. If, however, any one does not care to sing with me, what do I care? Let him howl for himself if he will.' The language of the apologia was restrained and moderate; though when it came to abuses in the Church Luther was combative against the 'many-headed monster, this inferno of simony, licentiousness, pomp, murder and other abominations in the Church'. 'Rome itself, yes, Rome, chief of all', he reminded the Pope, 'today derides good popes. For where in the Christian world are popes more ridiculed than in that authentic Babylon, Rome.' Here, perhaps, was a reminiscence of the former monastic tourist. 'I do not care', he ventured to say, 'what pleases or displeases the Pope. He is a man like other men. There have been many popes inclined to errors, vices, and even very strange things.' Lest such charges might seem to criticise that somewhat voluptuous Medici, Leo X, Luther declared that the reigning Pope was a man 'whose integrity and learning are a joy in the eyes of all good men'. 'Prostrate at the feet of your Holiness, I offer myself and all that I am and have. . . . Your voice I will recognise as the voice of Christ, who rules and speaks in you.' Was Luther really sincere in such sentiments? Like other men of similar temperament he was convinced that the truth of the arguments he was putting forward was so obvious that any reasonable Christian, among whom he doubtless at this time included the Pope, would be convinced of their validity. When they read his tract the Roman theologians must have felt uneasy at the ominous ring of self-assurance, of intellectual and spiritual conviction, even of pride, and of the confident faith, the product of long years of the study of theology and of personal tensions in the monastery at Wittenberg.

Luther's forthright statements naturally evoked a vigorous response in the German universities, where his attack on scholasticism was resented equally by nominalists and realists. 'I am absolutely convinced', he told his old tutor, Trutvetter, 'that it is impossible to reform the Church, unless the Cànon Laws, the decretals, the scholastic theology, philosophy, logic as they now are, are taken up by the roots, and other studies put in their place.' Few people can shew such strong emotional and often irrational reaction at criticism of their intellectual views as university dons. Luther and his opponents proved no exception to the general rule. The situation was further complicated by the rivalry which existed between his own order, the Augustinian Friars, and that of the Dominicans, of which Tetzel was a member. Tetzel issued a reasoned defence of his position from the University of Frankfort-on-Oder, a Dominican stronghold where one of the professors, Konrad Wimpina, took the lead in attacking Luther. Tetzel tried to show that Luther was questioning the authority of the Pope and so opening the road to ecclesiastical chaos; 'everyone will believe what pleases him'.

The authorities at Rome, hitherto dilatory, were spurred on by the Dominicans to take more direct action. The papal legate, Thomas de Vio, Cardinal of San Sisto, usually known as Cajetan, who was himself general of the Dominicans, attended the Imperial Diet which was meeting at Augsburg in 1518, avowedly if ironically to put an end to the Hussite heresy; but he took the opportunity to strengthen the understanding between the Pope and the German authorities. A specially blessed hat was given to the ailing Holy Roman Emperor, Maximilian. Albert of Mainz was made a cardinal, and the Elector of Saxony was promised the guerdon of the order of the Golden Rose and further indulgences for his collection of relics at Wittenberg. Meanwhile the auditor of the Sacred Palace, the Bishop of Ascoli, was ordered to summon Luther to Rome, and Sylvester Prierias was asked to answer the charges which Luther had made. His tract, hastily written in three days, was superficial and unconvincing.

Luther was undoubtedly worried by the moves which were being made to silence him, but he had no doubt whatever that the stand that he was making was approved by God. The difficulties and tensions of the past years seemed partly resolved through the challenge he had offered to the Church. The sermon which he had written in German on indulgences and grace had a wide sale. In another pamphlet he argued that a man unjustly excommunicated should not be debarred from the spiritual privileges of the Church. In his reply to the tract written by Prierias he hinted at the possibility of a General Council, a suggestion distinctly unwelcome to the Roman authorities, and illustrated his argument with reference to the crimes of Popes Julius II, Leo's predecessor, and Boniface VIII.

A new blow fell on August 7th, 1518, in the shape of a summons to Rome. Luther was to appear at Rome within 60 days to answer for the assertions that he had made in respect of papal supremacy and indulgences. Two days earlier the Emperor had himself reassured the papal legate that he would support such sentence as the Pope might give against Luther. On August 25th, 1518, the general of the Augustinians requested the Saxon provincial to secure the masterful friar's arrest. Similar instructions had been sent to Cardinal Cajetan, authorising him to employ the threat of full excommunication against such a 'child of evil' and to avail himself of secular assistance to procure Luther's seizure. Luther must by now have realised that the net was fast closing around him. Fully aware of the penalty that the Church meted out to recalcitrant heretics, he was naturally anxious and uneasy, but he showed no sign of a readiness to compromise. He recognised that his situation was perilous and that everything depended on the willingness of the Saxon Elector, a man whom he had never actually met, to defend him. He had, however, a very good friend in the Elector Frederick's chaplain, Spalatin, who persuaded Frederick that if the case was to be heard at all, it should be adjudged in Germany rather than at Rome. Specious excuses of weak health and the perils of travel were put forward to justify Luther's refusal to go to Rome; and as often with Luther depression gave way to exhilaration. 'I am not afraid!' he told Spalatin, '. . . for I am sure that everything that they are attacking comes to me from God.' Yet it was not easy for a single monk to withstand the concerted pressure of Church and State, and for Wittenberg to defy Rome.

Luther was indeed saved by the very fact that Church and State were not united. The support which the Elector had now decided to give to Luther's request and the comparatively dilatory tactics of the Roman authorities can only be understood within the context of the contemporary political scene. The reigning Emperor, Maximilian, was in poor health. There was every possibility of a new election to the Imperial throne in which Frederick of Saxony, as a member of the electoral college, and the Pope, as an interested participant in European power politics, were both keenly interested. The elderly Emperor favoured the claims of his grandson, Charles, the King of Spain. There were some who thought that the Elector of Saxony himself might be a candidate, and he, for his part, was being wooed by King Francis I of France. The Elector was indeed such a key figure that neither the Emperor, the German princes, the French King or the Pope would willingly alienate him. Pope Leo X, as a member of the Medici family, was especially anxious to secure the exclusion of King Charles. In such circumstances the affair of Luther seemed obviously of secondary importance. The papal officials decided that it would be more politic to win over the Elector by bribery than by threats. A Saxon curial official, Karl von Miltitz, told Spalatin that the Pope was ready to approve the grant of the Golden Rose to Frederick.

There were, however, other factors which for the moment made papal policy appear more conciliatory. Cajetan told the curial officials plainly that there was a mounting movement of criticism of ecclesiastical abuses in Germany, a demand for the reform of the Church and some downright anti-clericalism. It was decided that it was better not to press the charge demanding Luther's presence in Rome and instead to summons Luther to appear before Cajetan at Augsburg. While it could hardly be called a victory for Luther, at least the outcome was better than had a few weeks earlier seemed possible. He left for Augsburg feeling at once depressed and exulted. 'I clearly saw my grave ready and kept saying to myself, "What disgrace I shall be to my dear parents".' 'Only one thing is left', he had written to his fellow friar, Link, a few months earlier, on July 10th, 1518, 'a feeble and miserable broken body. If they take that away they will cut me off perhaps from one or two hours of life, but they cannot take away the soul. . . . I know that from the beginning the Word of Christ has been such that whoever wants to present it in the world must necessarily, like the Apostles, renounce everything and expect death at every hour. If this were not so, then it would not be the Word of Christ. It was brought with death, it has been spread abroad through the death of many. Manifold death may be necessary to it if it is to be preserved or brought back again.' Many of his friends believed that in going to Augsburg Luther was virtually signing his own death warrant.

Luther set out for Augsburg, accompanied by one of his fellow friars, towards the end of September, 1518. On his arrival he was lodged in the Carmelite monastery and was welcomed by the Saxon officials who must have strengthened his morale, weakened by depression as by the constipation which seemed to afflict him at moments of crisis. But his fears may well have been aroused when a member of the Cardinal's entourage, Urban of Serralonga, asked him acidly whether he supposed that the Elector would go to the length of actually fighting for his troublesome subject. Luther told the suave Italian that which he was to reiterate time and time again, that if what he was teaching was proved to be contrary to the true teaching of the Church, he would very readily recant. Luther's interlocutor, Cardinal Cajetan, was in some respect worthy of his opponent. He was a considerable scholar, who had been engaged for 15 years on a learned commentary in nine volumes on the works of Aquinas, a stern critic of existing abuses in the Church, and a man of exemplary life. It was unfortunate that Luther was by now convinced that Thomism and Scotism were two of the most insidious enemies of Christian teaching, as this obviously made it

12 Luther Preach

Detail of a painting in the Town Church, Wittenbe
by Lucas Cranach the El

Johannes Tetzel von Leipzig

13 John Tetzel
From an engraving by Brühl

14 John Eck
*From an anonymous
engraving*

difficult, other things apart, for the learned and pious Dominican to view his fellow friar sympathetically.

The meetings ultimately reaffirmed Luther's convictions. Where, Martin asked the Cardinal at their first conversation, lay the content of the heresy with which he was charged? The Cardinal replied that he had denied the validity of the doctrine of the treasury of merit of Christ and the saints upon which the system of indulgences rested, and that he had asserted that the efficacy of the sacrament was proportionate to the faith of its recipient. He tried to prove to Martin his error with a wealth of dialectic and learning, relying much on the bull issued by Clement VI in 1343 which had become a part of the canon law; but Martin was innately distrustful of the Cardinal's Thomistic approach. 'Although he may be a famous Thomist, he is a vague, obscure, and unintelligible theologian or Christian and therefore as unsuited to understand and judge the matter as an ass to play the harp.' Luther's judgments, to say the least, were always forthright. At the second interview, Luther was accompanied by Staupitz who had now arrived at Augsburg, but it proved equally inconclusive. Luther again declared that his teaching was in conformity with that of the Church and appealed to the universities of Basle, Freiburg, Louvain and Paris 'which from ancient days has been regarded as the most Christian university and most excellent in Holy Scriptures'. At the third and final meeting, Luther again denied that the treasury of merit had any foundation in Scripture and strongly supported the doctrine of the justification by faith. 'So long as the passages of the Scripture stand, I cannot do otherwise . . .' The Cardinal agreed to send a copy of Martin's statement to Rome but asked him to recant. '*Revoca*', he urged. There was an angry altercation, each in all probability saying more than discretion would have suggested. Luther was in fact doing the very thing that Urban of Serralonga had advised him against, indulging in dialectic with the Cardinal. At last Cajetan, unusually angry, told him imperiously: 'Go and do not return unless you are ready to recant.'

The conference at Augsburg had ended in an unpropitious stalemate. The legate, perhaps regretting his hasty if provoked outburst against Luther, summoned Staupitz and Link and urged them to get their friend to recant. The friar himself wrote in a propitiatory fashion, but the Saxons worried lest Cajetan might take precipitate action. 'I will not become a heretic,' Martin wrote, 'by contradicting the opinion with which I became a Christian: I will rather die, be burned, exiled, accursed.' He delayed in Augsburg a few days longer, perhaps

15 Augsburg. *From Schedel, 'Weltchronik', 1493*

awaiting another summons to the Cardinal's presence, writing a further justification of the stand he had taken, an appeal 'from the ill-informed' to the 'better-to-be-informed' Pope. This seems to have been affixed to the cathedral door on October 2nd, 1518, but Martin, perhaps fearing for his safety, had left the city two days previously. When he arrived at Nuremberg he learned of the existence of the papal order for his arrest, but he insisted that this must be a forgery. On October 31st, 1518, exactly a year after the posting of the theses which had set Germany by the ears, he re-entered the friendly city of Wittenberg.

This conference between Luther and Cajetan at Augsburg lacked the drama of later debates in which he was involved, but it nonetheless constituted a landmark in his career. Had Cajetan thought fit to break the safe-conduct and to have apprehended Luther, it is difficult to know what would have been the outcome; but he could hardly have made the attempt without the approval of the ailing Emperor and his own partner, the Cardinal of Gurk, who was not in Augsburg. Plainly Luther had revealed to his opponents the direction of his thoughts and his determination. Was it possible to keep him within the fold of the Church? Were his ideas a fundamental challenge to the dominant theology? Was there hope of a compromise? Would Luther himself come to terms? All these were questions which must have exercised the minds of educated men at the time. The issue was, however, not merely one which concerned Luther and the Church. It was affected by social and political issues which served to complicate further the future course of events. As Luther braced himself for the defence of his cause, and the Cardinal penned an elegant Latin account of the conference, neither could then have foreseen what the future had in store.

CHAPTER 4

The Making
of the Reformer

1518–1521

There is at least an element of historic inevitability about the course of events which ultimately resulted in the drama of the Diet of Worms. The situation in 1518 was clearly still fluid and with certain conditions an agreed solution might have been negotiated. The conditions, however, were palpably lacking. The Roman Church, not fully informed about the state of affairs, treated Luther with that peculiar blend of suave persuasion and authoritarian demand which it has often displayed towards those who have deviated from its teaching. In some respects Cajetan had been sweetly reasonable and he was later to be blamed for his moderation. On the other hand, Luther had taken an uncompromising position. In the following months argument was to be used relentlessly to bring him to yield, more especially through the medium of the great debate staged at Leipzig between Luther, Carlstadt and Eck. The curia brought its diplomatic charm to bear on the Elector; but behind the honeyed words there lay the threat of excommunication and the use of force. The Dominicans, hostile to Luther, did what they could to expedite his condemnation. In Germany itself the chief opposition to Luther came from a comparatively small group of university dons and churchmen, often as aware as Luther of the need for the reform of the Church, but outraged by his criticism of scholasticism and apprehensive of the threat to authority which his teaching implied.

Luther's own stand was prophetic in its vehemence and in its conviction. His critics indeed seemed only to make him the more intransigent. Since he had discarded the scholastic approach, though he still sometimes used the method of argument, he had to rebuild anew the structure of his faith, utilising the early Fathers, St. Augustine in particular, as well as the Bible itself. The more he perused the Scriptures the more convinced he became that their teaching had been corrupted by the Church. His mind was penetrating and agile. He read rapidly and intensively, using all the tools of contemporary grammatical science and philology to elucidate the meaning of the sacred text. The more he studied the more certain he became that the only fundamental authority for the Christian was the divinely inspired Word of God. He did not, however, equate the Word of God with the canon of Scripture. He had doubts about the authorship of the *Epistle to the Hebrews* (since the author declared that he had received the Gospel secondhand—ii, 3), and questioned the apostolic authority of James, Jude and the Apocalypse; but ultimately he subordinated his critical sense to his own evangelical experience. The power of the faith that justifies and the assurance of forgiveness of sins which it brought formed the foundation of his theology. His beliefs were rooted in Scripture; but even Scripture seemed subordinate to his experience.

This was the point of view from which he was henceforth to approach all the questions which were to confront him. When he attacked the power of human reason, he did so because reason was claiming more than was justified. Natural reason has its own sphere of competence but it can only surely apprehend the truths of revelation if it has been made 'captive to Christ'. Appropriate as the use of reason may be in the earthly kingdom, it is only of subordinate use in the spiritual

75

world. 'Without faith, reason is of no use and can do nothing. . . . But when illuminated, reason takes all its thoughts from the Word.' His attitude towards philosophy was much the same. He did not doubt its authenticity within its own sphere, but he claimed the schoolmen had been gravely mistaken in mingling it with theology. Yet his energies and even the authority of the Word of God were only fully unravelled in terms of his own decisive experience. 'Not Scripture only . . . but also experience. . . . Therefore, together with the Scripture I have the matter and experience.' Luther had no doubt that his experience was what he liked to call 'a laying hold upon Christ'. 'The true test by which to judge all books is to see whether they deal with Christ or not. . . . What does not teach Christ is not apostolic, even though St. Peter or Paul taught it.' Luther was convinced that he was 'preaching Christ'; he had the fervour, the divine illumination, the pragmatic authoritarianism of the prophet. It is, however, hardly surprising that his critics accused him of spiritual pride and egocentricity.

His theological conclusions were indeed in rapport with his psychological development as with the situation in which he found himself. Controversy had released him from the tedious routine of the monastic life for which he seemed in ways unsuited by nature. He had clearly found the conventual life of the Augustinian friar physically frustrating as well as spiritually unrewarding. It was not merely that he was justified by faith. He had also to justify himself to his companions and to himself. The quarrel in which he was now involved provided a perfect opportunity to escape the monotony of the friary. Some degree of *accidia* was intermingled with native egoism to make him find the theological conclusions to which his intellectual and spiritual development had led him strangely palatable. Even in 1518 there seems to have been very little hope that Luther could be effectively won over or that the Church, given its basic authoritarianism and illiberalism, could tolerate the challenge which Luther offered to its divinely grounded jurisdiction and testimony.

Contemporary circumstances, however, changed an insignificant dispute into a world-wide clash. The authority of the Church had been undermined by humanist writings, by anticlericalism, by the development of the secular powers and by national feeling. If Luther had been tried and executed as Hus had been in 1415, it is at least possible that his cause might have died with him; but each year that he survived aroused more and more support for his teaching in Germany. Every medieval controversy had given rise to a spate of pamphlets, but since each had to be copied by hand their circulation remained small and their final effectiveness as propaganda was very limited. The invention of the printing press had completely revolutionised the situation. Luther and his friends immediately realised the need for winning wider support by means of the printed word. Within 18 months of the original propositions made at Wittenberg in 1517 a stream of pamphlets issued from Luther's pen, which circulated widely in Germany and beyond the frontiers of the Empire.

The evidence as to the extent of early Lutheran propaganda is impressive indeed. The Basle publisher, Froben, printed an edition of Luther's Latin writings which was exhausted by the spring of 1519. Such editions were indeed small, but so was the learned and literate world which bought and read the books. The very fact that Latin was still the language of academic writing in all countries made it possible for interested scholars to read Luther's works in Paris or Pavia, Madrid or London. His German writings attracted a wider and possibly rather different public. In 1520 the Franciscan friar, Konrad Pellicanus, noted that his German works were on sale in Basle. There can be little doubt that he made articulate many of the complaints and fears which created dissatisfaction with the contemporary Church. Scholars such as Crotus Rubeanus, Wolfgang Capito and Ulrich von Hutten were attracted by the application of the humanists' criteria to the authority of the Church, and wrote to congratulate him on the stand he was taking and to promise him their support. Even Erasmus, who had greater reputation as a scholar than any other living man, at first expressed sympathetic interest. Academics who read his works were impressed by the pungency of his arguments and his intellectual penetration, if some were alarmed by the vehemence of his attacks on scholasticism. Churchmen expressed approval or indignation. Princes and nobles delighted in his forthright scurrility and apparent support for secular power against ecclesiastical authority. The merchant classes, long irritated by the Church's conservative attitude to usury and profit as by its financial demands, must have helped significantly in spreading Lutheran ideas in many a German town. The unschooled masses lay outside the range of his direct propaganda, but anti-clericalism was a potent force among the urban proletariat as well as among the peasantry; rumour which circulates with astonishing speed in illiterate societies must very soon have made popular the figure of the friar who had stood so courageously against the pride and pomp of prelacy. Luther was in fact drawing to himself many different strands of ill-feeling, doubtless accentuated by the wide prevalence of ecclesiastical abuses: anti-clericalism, German national feeling, intellectual novelty, bourgeois interests, spiritual aspirations. 'All Switzerland, Constance, Augsburg and a good part of Italy depend on Luther', Lasius told Mutianus in December, 1519. It was probably an exaggeration but in the circumstances pardonable.

A period of comparative quiet followed Luther's departure from Augsburg. Von Miltitz's attempt to conciliate the Elector and even Luther himself had been for the moment side-tracked because of the more pressing problem of an imminent Imperial election. Luther was busy writing his own account of the meeting with Cajetan at Augsburg and, in spite of the Elector's advice to restrain his pen, had ventured to suggest that a General Council of the Church should be summoned. He was now confronted with a new and able opponent in Dr. Eck of Ingolstadt. Eck, who was a genuine scholar skilled in the cut and thrust of academic debate, opposed Luther's teaching on indulgences, and was so much involved in dispute with Luther and his colleague at Wittenberg, Andreas Carlstadt, that the disputants asked the theological faculty of the University of Leipzig and Duke George of Saxony for permission to stage a public disputation. The Leipzig theologians and the Bishop of Merseburg, Adolf of Anhalt, were lukewarm but the Duke, a keen amateur theologian who had once studied for the priesthood and who was besides eager to raise the prestige of his leading city, welcomed the plans for what might well prove an entertaining as well as edifying academic circus.

The disputation at Leipzig turned out to be more edifying than entertaining. Eck's theses, published on December 29th, 1518, were directed straightly at Luther's views; the good man is not in mortal sin; souls in purgatory may be freed through the 'treasury of merit'; the Pope as the successor of Peter and the Vicar of Christ is entitled to make use of this treasury. Luther repeated his opinions on penance and forgiveness, and put forward the most radical criticism of the papal claims that he had yet expounded: 'That the Roman Church is superior to all others is shown by the vapid decrees which the Roman popes have promulgated during four hundred years; against these are the historical evidence of fifteen hundred years, the text of the Sacred Scriptures, and the decree of the Council of Nicaea, the most sacred of all.' He was even more outspoken to Spalatin, writing: 'I am busy with the papal decrees for my disputation , and (for your ear alone) I don't know whether the Pope is Antichrist himself or his apostle, so wretchedly is Christ, that is, the truth, twisted, and crucified by him in the decrees.' While Duke George and the Leipzig authorities had been ready to admit Carlstadt as a disputant, they were less eager to welcome Luther and it was only at Eck's behest that they agreed to sponsor the invitation.

On June 24th, 1519, a motley band of Wittenbergers, Luther, Carlstadt, the Rector of the University, Duke Barnim of Pomerania, Melanchthon and a dozen or so professors and jurists in wagons (the one in which Carlstadt was travelling lost its wheel outside St. Paul's Church and threw the theologian), with a number of students armed with halberds and spears running beside their leaders, entered the Grimma gate of Leipzig. Eck, together with the Duke of Bavaria and representatives of the wealthy banking house of Fugger, had already arrived. The Bishop vainly tried to stop the debate which very nearly came to grief over procedural difficulties. At last these were smoothed out and on the morning of June 27th, 1518, the ducal officials, the leading representatives of the university and city, together with the disputants and their followers were welcomed at the university by Simon Pistorius before they went into procession to St. Thomas' Church for a solemn mass sung by 12 voices.

The debate began the same afternoon and lasted until July 15th, 1518, when the Duke wanted the hall for a guest. Eck showed himself to be a singularly shrewd and skilled debater, and had comparatively little difficulty in scoring off Carlstadt. Luther took the rostrum on July 4th, carrying a little bunch of fresh pinks which he smelled from time to time, a characteristically sensitive and romantic gesture. As usual he expressed his respect for the Pope, but defended the statements that he had made about papal authority by reference to the Fathers and to the Scriptures. On the second day of the debate with Luther, Eck charged Luther with repeating the pestilential and condemned errors of Wyclif and Hus. This was a pertinent thrust, not least because the Leipzigers, whose university had been founded as a result of the resistance of the Bohemian Germans to the Czech followers of Hus, held the Hussites in particular detestation. Luther at first denied the accusation indignantly, asserting that he was simply disputing the apostolic character of the Petrine supremacy and repudiating the suggestion that he was fostering a schism. Yet Eck had effectively cornered his opponent. Luther felt obliged to confess that he believed that some of the articles which Hus promoted were 'plainly very Christian and evangelical which it is not possible for the universal Church to condemn', among them the statement which declared that it is unnecessary for salvation to believe that the Roman Church is superior to all others. 'Whether', Luther stoutly asserted, 'it be of Wyclif or Hus, I do not care. I know that Gregory Nazanzenus, Basil the Great, Epiphanian the Cyprian, and innumerable other Greek bishops were saved, who nevertheless did not believe in this article, nor is it in the power of the Roman pope or the inquisitors into heresy to found new articles of faith but to judge according to those already established. It is not possible for a faithful Christian to be constrained beyond Sacred Scripture, which was properly established by divine Law, unless a new revelation has been established.' In making such a statement, Luther provided for his opponent a renewed opportunity to reiterate the charge of Hussitism and to suggest that he denied the authority of the Council of Constance. The friar intervened passionately: 'I protest before you all and publicly that the excellent doctor in speaking thus about me is an impudent liar.'

Feeling was evidently beginning to run high. In the next session the President, Cäsar Pflug, reminded the contestants and their followers that they must refrain from recrimination and abuse. Luther continued to repeat that it was not necessary for salvation to believe that the Roman Church was superior to all others and to deny the divine foundation of the Petrine supremacy; but equally he declared that he was not challenging the primacy of Peter or the necessity of obedience to it. Again Eck insisted that Luther had challenged the authoritative decrees of the Council of Constance and, thus provoked, Martin agreed that even a council could err if it sanctions what is not in agreement with the Word of God. Eck must have sighed with relief as Luther made this admission since he had gone some way to establish his heterodoxy. He had denied the apostolic foundation of the Petrine headship. He had now asserted the errancy of general councils. 'I will tell you, honoured father, if you say that a council, properly convoked, can err and has erred, you are for me a heathen and a publican.'

The genuine cleavage of opinion must by now have been obvious to all those who were listening to the debate long before Johann Lambergius made his lengthy closing oration to a near-empty hall. It was soon to be clear to German, indeed European opinion that Luther had challenged the papal authority on fundamental points. There could henceforth be relatively little hope of a real compromise. Eck and the Dominicans brought increasing pressure to bear on the tardy curial officials and at last Pope Leo agreed to the publication of the bull, *Exsurge Domine*, dated June 15th, 1520, which condemned 41 propositions from Luther's writings as 'heretical or scandalous or offensive to pious ears'; subsequently his books were burned in the Piazza Navona at Rome. Eck, his travelling expenses paid by the papal exchequer, hurried back from Rome to Germany, fortified by what must have seemed a complete victory over his opponent. He was followed northward by the Roman diplomat and humanist scholar, Hieronymus Aleander, who was entrusted with the difficult task of persuading the young new Emperor, Charles V, and the Imperial Diet, to support papal policy. The way was now clear for the summons to Worms.

In fact, Luther was extremely busy with his pen in the period which intervened between the ending of the debate at Leipzig and his summons to attend the Diet of Worms. His writings formed such significant propaganda and so clearly indicate the comparatively radical position that he had by now come to occupy that they demand some attention. The first, *The Address to the Christian Nobility of the German Nation*, was a virulent attack on papal power, and an appeal, in part founded on nascent German national feeling, to the laity to rise against a foreign priesthood. He asserted that the Roman Church was encircled by three walls: the claim of the ecclesiastical power to be superior to the temporal, the Pope's assumption that he alone has the authority to interpret the Scriptures, and the right to call a Council (which is ultimately subservient to him). These 'walls' ought to be broken down, for they are constructed on indefensible foundations. All power, temporal as much as spiritual, originates with God, nor does Scripture support the conclusion that the spirituality should be treated differently from the temporalty. 'If a priest is slain, the land is put under an interdict: why not also if a peasant is slain?' He tilted at those who propounded the inerrancy of the Pope. He is as much a man as other men and as liable to temptation. There can be no authority for confining the interpretation of the Scriptures to the Pope. 'It is a wickedly devised fable—and they cannot quote a single letter to confirm it—that it is, for the Pope alone to interpret the Scriptures or to confirm the interpretation of them. They have assumed the authority of their own selves. And though they say that this was authority given to St. Peter when the keys were given to him, it is plain enough that the keys were not given to St. Peter alone, but to the whole community.' He dismisses as abruptly the claim that the Pope has alone the right to convoke a General Council of the Church; 'they can show nothing in the Scriptures giving the Pope sole power to call and confirm councils; they have nothing but their own laws; but these hold good only so long as they are not injurious to Christianity and the laws of God'. If the need arises, and if the Pope himself is a cause of offence to the Church, 'a faithful member of the whole body must do what he can to procure a true free council'.

He then discussed the various abuses which afflicted the Church: the luxurious living and the ceremonial pomp of the Pope and the cardinals of his court and the ruinous conditions of churches and monasteries which resulted from these things. 'There is such a swarm of vermin at Rome, all called papal, that Babylon itself never saw the like. There are more than three thousand papal secretaries alone. . . . Who can count the "servants" of the Pope and his cardinals, seeing that if he goes out riding, he is attended by three or four thousand mule-riders, more than any king or emperor?' 'What is the use in Christendom of the people called "cardinals"? I will tell you. In Italy and Germany there are many rich convents, endowments, fiefs, and benefices, and as the best way of getting these into the hands of Rome, they created cardinals and gave them sees, convents and prelacies, and thus destroyed the service of God. That is why Italy is almost a desert now: the convents are destroyed, the sees consumed, the revenues of the prelacies, and of all the churches drawn to Rome: towns are decayed, the country and the people ruined, because there is no more any worship of God or preaching; why? Because the cardinals must have all the wealth. No Turk could have thus desolated Italy and overthrown the worship of God.' These exaggerated comments, read by men who had never visited Italy, were intended to suggest that what was Italy's fate would sooner or later be the destiny of Germany. 'Now that Italy is sucked dry, they come to Germany.'

Luther concentrated much of his attention on the financial demands of the Papacy, criticising the use of annates, the sale of the pallium, the employment of the banking house of Fugger and the system of papal reservation of benefices. The Germans were being pauperised by the export of gold to Rome to pay for the un-Christian policies and way of living of the papal court and its emissaries. 'If we justly hang thieves and behead robbers, why do we leave the greed of Rome so unpunished, that is the greatest thief and robber that has appeared or can appear on earth and does all this in the holy name of Christ and St. Peter?' He believes that the time has come for an end to be put to such evils. 'It would be no wonder, if God were to rain sulphur and fire from heaven and cast Rome down into the pit, as He did formerly to Sodom and Gomorrah. . . . Oh noble princes and sirs, how long will you suffer your lands and your people to be the prey of these ravening wolves?'

The remedies which he proposed were a strange admixture of the trivial and the significant. Bishops should refuse to pay annates nor should they be allowed to fetch their palliums from Rome. Appeals should be heard in Germany rather than in Italy. The practice of papal provisions and reservations should be abolished. Pilgrimages in general, and to Rome in particular, should cease, for 'the nearer Rome, the worse Christians'. Indulgences and similar abuses should be eliminated: 'if you are to ride to heaven on his wax and parchment your wagon will soon break down and you will fall into hell.' He asserted that parish priests should be free to marry: 'there is many a poor priest free from blame in all other respects, except that he has succumbed to human frailty and come to shame with a woman, both minded in their hearts to live together always in conjugal fidelity. . . . It is not every priest that can do without a woman, not only on account of human frailty, but still more for his household.' He would abolish saints' days: 'my reason is this: with our present abuses of drinking, gambling, idling and all manner of sin, we vex God more on holy days than on others . . . the common man . . . loses a day's work, and he spends more than usual, besides weakening his body and making himself unfit for labour.' He demanded a reform of the curriculum of universities and schools, with greater emphasis on the teaching of Scripture and the banishment of the philosophical works of Aristotle and of canon law from the syllabus. 'I am in great anxiety lest the universities become open doors of hell, if they do not give training in the Holy Scriptures and drive them into young people.'

In two respects Luther's criticisms were fundamental. He praised the Hussites, but did not necessarily support their teaching. He did, however, lambast the papal office with devastating virulence and once again raised the familiar medieval spectacle of the Pope as Antichrist. 'Dost thou hear this, O Pope! not the most holy, but the most sinful? Would that God would hurl thy chair headlong from heaven, and cast it down into the abyss of hell! Who gave you the power to exalt yourselves above your God; to break and to loose what He has commanded; to teach Christians, more especially Germans, who are of noble nature, and are famed in all histories for uprightness and truth, to be false, unfaithful, perjured, treacherous and wicked? God has commanded to keep faith and observe oaths even with enemies; you dare to cancel this command; laying it down in your heretical, anti-Christian decretals that you have power to do so; through your mouth and your pen Satan lies as he never lied before, teaching you to twist and pervert the Scriptures according to your own arbitrary will . . . the man of sin and the child of damnation.' Luther hinted that the remedy for this state of affairs might lie in the summons of a General

Council; 'now may God so help a free council that it may teach the Pope that he too is a man, not above God, as he makes himself out to be.'

The Address to the Christian Nobility was a deliberate attempt to win partisans for what was in process of becoming an insurgent movement against the established Church. The theological foundations upon which Luther founded his ideas were played down; the appeal to Scripture and the stress on justification by faith played a comparatively small part in the argument. This was in part because Luther was addressing the educated laity rather than the informed clergy. They were much more likely to be affected by suggestive charges which touched them or their property personally. Luther reiterated the danger that the papal policy represented to their property and to their pockets. 'What has brought us Germans to such a pass that we have to suffer this robbery and this destruction of our property by the Pope?' The *Address* was an intelligent appeal to self-interest. By implication Luther made it plain that the temporal power was equal to the spiritual, if not its superior. 'Let it be decreed that no temporal matter shall be submitted to Rome, but all shall be left to the jurisdiction of the temporal authorities.' 'The Pope should have no power over the Emperor, except to anoint and crown him at the altar.' 'All these excessive, over-presumptuous, and most wicked claims of the Pope are the invention of the devil, with the object of bringing in Antichrist in due course and of raising the Pope above God. . . . It is not meet that the Pope should exalt himself above temporal authority, except in spiritual matters, such as preaching and absolution.' He made an implicit appeal to the Germanism of his readers: 'Let us rouse ourselves, fellow Germans.' He did not ignore the moral failings of his own people, but they compared favourably with those of the contemptible Italians.

In some respects in spite of its outspoken criticisms the pamphlet's argument was basically conservative. It was not the first time that the Pope had been identified with Antichrist or that the curia had been as harshly criticised, and that too by orthodox churchmen. Ardent supporters of the Imperialist cause had been quite as forthright in their denunciation of abuses. The tract could have been written almost at any time in the past 400 years. Circumstances rather than language made it significant. Where formerly it could only have circulated in a limited and tardy fashion, the printing press brought it quickly to the notice of a wide public whilst its arguments were still very relevant. It was designedly written in German rather than in Latin. It made articulate complaints and grievances that had existed for generations but which had rarely been put with such cogency or with such appeal to personal interests in recent times.

No sooner had Luther issued one broadside than another, different in its character and addressed to a dissimilar audience, appeared. *The Babylonian Captivity of the Church*, written in Latin rather than in German, was a theological work addressed primarily to the clergy. It was designed to show how the Church had been made captive through the sinister policy of the Roman clergy and their head, who had deliberately deceived the faithful to preserve the vested interests of the kingdom of Babylon. More especially they have taught that there are seven sacraments, of which only three, baptism, penance and the Eucharist, can be regarded as valid, and have misinterpreted them to serve their own evil cause. Thus whereas Jesus Christ, as the Scriptures teach, summoned laity and clergy alike to drink of the one cup, the priests have reserved the chalice to their own use, thus depriving the Christian laity of what is theirs by Christ's own teaching. They have also taught that the bread and wine of the Eucharist are simply the 'accidents' of the sacrament, which is an invention of the Aristotelian philosopher perpetuated by Thomas Aquinas and the schoolmen. While he criticised the doctrine of transubstantiation, he did not deny that Christ was really and truly present in the sacrament; using an image previously employed by Wyclif among other writers he stated that God is in the bread and wine as fire is in hot iron. He declared that the efficacy of the sacrament is proportionate to the faith of the believer, and asserted that it could not be regarded as a good work in itself. In his challenge to the sacrificial interpretation of the Mass, repeating arguments that he already put forward in his sermon on the Mass, he went some way to undermine the sacramental foundation of the priesthood and the Church. Why, he asked, should the Mass not be performed in Greek, Hebrew, German or any other language?

He questioned contemporary teaching on baptism, especially the belief in a quasi-mechanical or magical action of the sacrament. Faith was the great desideratum, since faith in baptism is such that even the power of sin is impotent to circumvent it. 'This knowledge of baptism is today a captive, and to whom can we ascribe this fact, save to the single tyrant, the Roman pontiff.' The Pope has corrupted the true meaning of the baptismal rite by the forms and ceremonies with which he has invested it. The Pope, he repeated, must be regarded as a 'man of sin and the son of perdition, who sits in the Church like God and by his doctrines and statutes increases the sin of the Church and the

THE MAKING OF THE REFORMER

destruction of souls'; his kingdom is 'nothing but the dominion of
Babylon and the true Antichrist'.

In similar fashion he charged Rome with distorting the true meaning of the sacrament of penance by dividing it into the formal cate-
gories of contrition, confession and absolution, scholastic subtleties
which effectively eliminate the element of true repentance. He thinks
that there is something to be said for confession but argues that it has
become an instrument abused for its own interest by a tyrannising
priesthood. In any case the attempt to create a mechanical balance
sheet by grading sins and penances according to their assumed serious-
ness is completely unjustified by the teaching of Scripture.

The remaining sacraments lack scriptural foundation. Confirmation,
which may be termed a sacramental rite rather than a genuine
sacrament, has become a device to strengthen episcopal authority.
Although marriage is of divine institution, it cannot be regarded as a
sacrament. He condemned vigorously the Roman practice of dispensation and annulment. 'There is no impediment (to marriage) today
which the intercession of mammon does not legitimise, so that the
laws of man seem to have been produced for no other reason than that
such avaricious men and rapacious Nimrods should have snares for
money and nooses for souls.' In his anger at the man-made obstacles
created by the vested interests of the priesthood, he advanced uncon-
ventional suggestions, such as, for instance, that a woman who has an
impotent husband should be entitled to cohabit with another (provided he is unmarried) and rear his children. Under divine law such a
woman must be regarded as free; yet he attacked divorce, intimating
that even bigamy was preferable. Here may be descried hints of the
attitude which he was later to take towards the matrimonial difficulties of Philip of Hesse. He objected to calling ordination a sacrament
because it placed the priesthood in an unjustified position of privilege.
In fact baptism must make priests of all men if rightly received. Extreme unction, which he believed to be founded on the dubious
teaching of St. James, though abused by the Church, is in itself harmless, though not divinely instituted.

Shortly after the publication of the *Babylonian Captivity*, Luther
issued in October, 1520, another small tract, written first in Latin and
then translated into German, *On the Freedom of a Christian Man*.
The work was prefaced by an open letter to the Pope couched in
conciliatory terms. He praised Pope Leo X as a man but castigated the
system of which he was the victim. 'For many years now, nothing else
has overflowed from Rome into the world—as you are not ignorant—

16   The Pope as Antichrist
From a drawing by Melchior Lorch

The Pope is depicted with a tail and other bestial attributes of Satan. The frogs coming from his mouth relate to the description of Antichrist in Revelation, xvi, 13—'And I saw three unclean spirits like frogs come out of the mouth of the false prophet'. The drawing was dedicated to Luther.

17 'A Table of the Bussop of Rome, the Four Evangelists casting stone
at him.'

*From a Flemish painting, time of Henry VIII; reproduced
by gracious permission of H.M. The Queen*

than the laying waste of goods, of bodies, and of souls, and the worst examples of all the worst things. These things are dearer than light to all men; and the Church of Rome, formerly the most holy of all churches, has become the most lawless den of thieves, the most shameless of all brothels, the very kingdom of sin, death and hell; so that not even Antichrist, if he were to come could devise any addition to its wickedness.'

By and large, however, the *Freedom of a Christian Man* sounded a very different note, reflecting that other side of Luther's personality which his polemic so often concealed, revealing a man who was deeply devout and profoundly aware of the meaning of Christian vocation. The tract was unusually free from the strident and occasionally egotistical bombast which marked so much of his polemic writing. It was a piece of popular theology addressed to the common reader on the necessity and virtue of faith. He began with the Pauline paradox that: 'A Christian man is the most free lord of all, and subject to none; a Christian man is the most dutiful subject of all, and subject to everyone.' There is, Luther avowed, a duality in man's nature 'spiritual and bodily', spirit and flesh. The health of the former, the inward or spiritual man, the means by which 'a man becomes justified, free and a true Christian', is a prior necessity, for 'What can it profit the soul that the body should be in good condition, free and full of life . . . when even the most impious slaves of every kind of vice are prosperous in these matters?'

The Word of God gives life to the soul of man. If it responds to this, then 'it is rich and wants for nothing, since that is the word of life, of truth, of light, of peace, of justification, of salvation, of joy, of liberty, of wisdom, of virtue, of grace, of glory, and of every good thing'. But what is the Word of God? It is the 'Gospel of God, concerning His Son, incarnate, risen and glorified, through the Spirit, the Sanctifier', and above all it is faith in Christ. 'For faith alone, and the efficaciousness of the Word of God, bring salvation.' 'The Word of God cannot be received and honoured by any works, but by faith alone. Hence it is clear that as the soul needs the Word alone for life and justification, so it is justified by faith alone, and not by any works.' It is this which confers the forgiveness of sins, that assured sense of spiritual re-birth and the possibility of salvation. The Scripture is divided into precepts and promises. The precepts teach man what is good, show him what he ought to do but do not give him the power to accomplish it. But the promises of God declared: 'If you wish to fulfil the law, and, as the law requires not to covet, lo! believe in Christ, in whom is promised to

you grace, justification, peace and liberty.' The influence of the teaching of St. Paul in his Epistles to the Romans and the Galatians is
everywhere manifest. 'No good works, not even all good works put
together, can compare with it, since no work can cleave to the word of
God or be in the soul. Faith alone and the word reign in it; such as is
the word, such is the soul made by it, just as iron exposed to fire glows
like fire, on account of its union with the fire. It is clear then that to a
Christian man his faith suffices for everything, and that he has no
need of works for justification.' Faith then confers victory, salvation
and redemption, and unites the believer to Christ, as the wife is
united to her husband. Christ 'by the wedding ring of faith, takes a
share in the sins, death and hell of His wife, nay, makes them His
own, and deals with them not otherwise than as if they were His,
and as if He Himself had sinned'. 'The mystical union wrought between Christ and the believing soul must bring not merely peace of
mind and inward joy but the power, the capacity to vanquish sin which
the Christian had hitherto lacked.' 'From all these considerations'
then 'any one may clearly see how a Christian man is free from all
things; so that he needs no works in order to be justified and saved,
but receives these gifts in abundance from faith alone. Nay, were he
so foolish as to pretend to be justified, set free, saved, and made a
Christian, by means of any good work, he would immediately lose
faith, with all its benefits. Such folly is prettily represented in the
fable where a dog, running along in the water and carrying in his
mouth a real piece of meat, is deceived by the reflection of the meat
in the water, and, in trying with open mouth to seize it, loses the meat
and its image at the same time.'

Luther, however, did not mean to convey that works had no place
in the Christian scheme of things. He was no antinomian. 'Good
works', he insisted, 'do not make a good man, but a good man does
good works', just as 'Bad works do not make a bad man, but a bad
man does bad works.' A Christian, consecrated by his faith in Christ,
will perform good works; but the good works do not make him a
better Christian. 'That is the effect of faith alone, nay, unless he
were previously a believer and a Christian, none of his works
would have any value at all, they would really be impious and
damnable sins.' Good works are by themselves of no account but they
are the natural and indeed necessary effects of faith. 'As works do not
make a believing man, so neither do they make a justified man; but
faith as it makes a man a believer and justified, so also it makes
his works good.' 'It is a little booklet', Luther commented on *The*

Freedom of a Christian Man, 'so far as paper is concerned, but if its meaning is understood, it contains the whole sum of a Christian life.'

These three dissimilar tracts, cumulatively, revealed the real cleavage that then existed between Luther and the Church. The papal bull of condemnation, *Exsurge Domine,* which was beginning to circulate inside Germany, stressed the peril of the 'deadly poison' that the fox, Luther, was spreading in the vineyard. He was exhorted to obey the Church, to recant formally or to come to Rome. He was again given a grace period of 60 days after which he and his followers would be condemned as obstinate heretics. He was ordered to abstain from preaching or writing in the intervening period; and his books should be burned. If it was possible, he himself should be detained; those who sheltered him were liable to severe punishment. While the bull was to be published throughout Germany, it must be posted especially on the doors of the cathedral churches of Brandenburg, Meissen and Merseburg, the three dioceses geographically contiguous to Wittenberg. In reply Luther issued a vituperative pamphlet, a familiar blend of theological penetration and scathing abuse, which had a wide sale. Yet could the war of words remain that alone? Luther, nervous, sensitive but spurred on by an inner dynamic, showed no sign of yielding. The Church in Germany was far from united in its disapproval; the papalists were mustering their supporters.

Hitherto the papal policy had been comparatively ineffectual because papal politics had acted as an essential brake on religious decisions. The Pope had not wished to prevent a favourable outcome to the Imperial election. Now that the young Hapsburg, Charles V, had been elected in spite of papal diplomacy, it was virtually essential to make the best of a bad job. The publication of the papal bull of condemnation showed, however, that the curia could no longer tolerate the existence of its truculent antagonist. It decided that it must authorise its legate, Aleander, to publish the bull and to negotiate with the Emperor and the Imperial Diet so as to ensure Luther's proscription. The legate, Girolamo Aleander, a Venetian by birth, was a good Greek scholar who had worked with Erasmus at the Aldine Press and who had served as Rector of the University of Paris; but he was also an administrator (who had acted as chancellor to the wily Bishop of Liège), a diplomat (who had been papal secretary and librarian at Rome) as well as a suave and attractive man of the world (his interest in von Hutten's cure for syphilis was not merely academic). While there was little doubt about his ability, by temperament and training he was likely to be antipathetic to Luther; nor was he the sort of man whom Luther would himself respect.

His various qualities made him, however, a good choice for bringing the papal condemnation of Luther to the notice of the Germans, though his work seemed initially to meet with limited success. He decided that one of the most spectacular ways of underlining Luther's heterodoxy was to arrange a public burning of his books, conducted with due ceremonial and in the presence of the leading representatives of Church, University and State. First, however, he had to present the papal bull to the young Emperor, which he did at Antwerp on September 26th, 1520. He could then with Imperial approval carry out the work of incineration. He began at Louvain (on October 8th) in the market square, went on to Liège, thence to Cologne (where he succeeded in having two interviews with the Elector Frederick who characteristically stone-walled) and finally to Mainz where the executioner at first obstinately refused to light the fire and the crowd began to pelt the Italian with stones. Indeed the more Aleander travelled about Germany, the more aware he became of the growing support for Luther and of the extent to which the curia had underestimated the danger. The university authorities at Louvain began to regret the approval that they had given to the burning of his books. At Cologne Aleander had been embarrassingly aware of the latent hostility of the powerful knight, Franz von Sickingen, at whose nearby castle of Ebernburg there was living the humanist versifier, Ulrich von Hutten, a more intransigent opponent of Roman claims than Luther himself.

He must too have learned with indignation of the way in which the papal bull had been greeted at Wittenberg. On the evening of December 9th, 1520, Melanchthon had affixed a notice to the church door urging all who cherished evangelical truth to gather at nine the next morning before the church of the Holy Cross (just outside the Elster Gate). Here a bonfire was made into which were thrown papal decrees, volumes of the canon law and the *Summa Angelica* of Angelo of Chiavasso. Amidst shouts of jubilation Luther himself flung the bull which had condemned him, declaring: 'Because you have condemned the truth of God, He also condemns you today to the fire, amen.' As the paper blazed and the smoke rose high in the sky the crowd sang a *Te Deum*. Later in the day the students arranged their own celebration to the sound of music and revelry, with less emphasis on the religious aspect of the event. Thus in a theatrical demonstration that was half-way between an academic occasion and a university bump supper, Luther metaphorically burned his boats behind him. He had symbolically destroyed not merely the papal bulls and decrees but the canon law on which the authority of the Church rested. The flame that lit the wintry day would not slowly die.

If Luther had no intention of compromise, his critics were less united than Aleander had hoped. The young Emperor, Charles V, devout, immature and yet aware of the great responsibility which rested on his shoulders, would not readily take precipitate action without consulting with his advisers. Many of these were churchmen but they were cautious men, suspicious of papal policy and ultimately more concerned with protecting their master's authority than preserving the Church against the attacks of a renegade friar. It is doubtful whether they were much better informed than the curia about the degree of support that Luther had won in Germany. They were, however, quite clear that it would be impolitic to alienate his patron, the Elector of Saxony. It was he who really stood between Luther and the Emperor's decision to implement the papal bull. In spite of his following, the professor depended for his freedom on the will of this cautious, stolid and sensible Saxon prince. The latter suggested that the Emperor should himself interview Luther. The negotiations which were thus initiated were prolonged and complicated. It was very far from clear when the Emperor arrived at Worms for the opening of the Imperial Diet on January, 1521, that a momentous meeting between the two men which was to affect the future history of Europe was soon to take place.

CHAPTER 5

The Diet of Worms

1521

The Diet of Worms might well appear as the climacteric of Luther's career, and in a sense it was so, since as a result of his meeting with the Emperor Charles V the latter decided to implement the papal decision. As a result the principal secular and ecclesiastical authorities combined to stamp out the challenge to their order. The drama of the ensuing situation has so gripped the historians' imagination that the importance of the Diet itself has been sometimes obscured. In effect there can be little doubt that the conclusions of the debate were more or less inevitable. There was no reason to suppose that Luther would compromise or withdraw his extensive condemnation of the Pope and the papal hierarchy, his criticism of the sacramental theology of the Church and of the demand that he put forward for the doctrine of justification by faith and for the individual to accept the authority of the Word of God. Similarly the Roman Church could not condone the criticisms that Luther had made without violating its divine function and purpose. In fact the outward causes of complaint, the worldliness of the clergy, the corruption to which the Church had fallen victim, the question of indulgences itself, were really peripheral matters which confused the real issues dividing the Catholic from the Lutheran. The Church could, and would, put its house in order, cleanse its Augean stables, root out its abuses and clarify its doctrine; but it could not accept the challenge which Luther offered to the Petrine authority of the Pope or to its sacramentally-founded theology.

The less perceptive observers were almost certainly more impressed by the abuses which had for so long been held up to criticism than by doctrinal deviations. The power, pretensions and pomp of the clerical order, the gap that there seemed to be between what was taught and what was practised, had for centuries created a feeling of contempt for and hostility towards the Church among all classes of society (as well as among some of the thinking clergy), though perhaps more specifically among the industrious merchants and the workers in town and country, who felt and resented the financial demands made upon them by the Church. Contemporaneously the lay princes cast envious eyes on ecclesiastical wealth and property. Anti-clericalism was a powerful factor in creating support for Luther; but anti-clericalism was not necessarily associated with a doctrinal revolution. Only a minority of those who cheered Luther as he moved towards Worms and who cast surly glances at the papal legate, understood the meaning of justification by faith or would have readily embraced Luther's theology; but they were very well aware that Luther had defied the Pope and had attacked the Church's vested interests. When Aleander told the Pope that nine-tenths of the Germans supported Luther, he meant that they were opposed to Rome, and that Luther was the spear-head of anti-papalism.

The comparative confusion which must have existed in 1520–1 as to the things for which Luther stood or was supposed to stand explains the importance of the Diet of Worms. It made possible the rise of a middle party, composed of all those who wished to divest the Church in some degree of its power, privileges and property, to reform it of its abuses but who were not especially concerned with modifying or changing its theology. These were the men who were ready, as the Emperor's confessor, Father Glapion, told Ulrich von Hutten, to praise Luther's early attacks on the corruption in the Church and the scandal of indulgences, but who could not go with him in his more radical attacks on the authority of the Pope. Unwilling to surrender Luther to the papal agents, this group wanted the Emperor to adopt Fabian tactics in dealing with the legate, hoping that a compromise could be ultimately arranged which would prevent the fragmentation of the Church. They were Erasmian in their sympathies and numbered, as Aleander regretfully noted, some of the Emperor's prominent advisers. They were, perhaps, insufficiently homogeneous to found a party, but their appearance at the Diet of Worms did much to determine the next 30 years of German history. They would not admit that the break between Lutherans and Catholics was incapable of solution, and their activity, rather than that of Luther himself, lies behind all the various councils, diets and conferences which, like modern disarmament conferences, met with monotonous if futile regularity in the ensuing years.

The young Emperor, Charles V, was the centre of all hopes. He was then in his twenty-first year, the master of a great unwieldy dominion, in character stolid, genuine, conscientious, not especially intelligent or outstandingly capable, more sensible than he looked, by no means a great man, but possessing an underlying strength and a sense of duty which carried him through the next three decades until ill-health and political disillusion led him to retire to the solitary luxury of a house attached to the Hieronymite monastery of Yuste in Spain. He had been subject since his early years to the influence of Flemish nobles and churchmen, like Chièvres and Adrian Dedel (who was shortly to succeed to the papal throne as Adrian VI), but he was not a tool or the voice of a faction; perhaps the most influential member of his entourage was to be an Erasmian churchman, Mercurino Gattinara. In spite of his youth Charles had already enjoyed a wide political experience. Succeeding in 1516 in his sixteenth year to his grandfather's throne of Aragon, he had arrived in Spain to find it surging with revolt; but, after making some initial mistakes resulting from his political immaturity and his trust in his Flemish advisers, he had displayed considerable shrewdness in bringing about a restoration of royal authority once the revolt had collapsed. This was hardly his personal responsibility, for his attention had then been focused on his newly-won Imperial position. Although the effective power of the Holy Roman Emperor was singularly limited, the prestige attached to the office was still enormous. The negotiations which preceded the election were criss-crossed with self-interest, as the Electors feathered their nests, and the Pope tried to prevent the election of the young Hapsburg prince. Charles' conduct of the complex bargaining which led to his eventual election as Emperor in 1519 showed some political insight. As Emperor his wealth and power came from his hereditary possessions, the Spanish empire, the Low Countries and his Austrian territories, rather than from the amorphous conglomeration of principalities, free cities, bishops and other semi-autonomous authorities which made up the empire in Germany. He went, fresh from the splendours of the traditional ceremonial of his coronation at Aachen, to the ardours and archaic procedure of the Imperial Diet which was meeting at Worms. Charles was not a true German but a Burgundian; his knowledge of history, as his religious convictions, was rooted less in Spanish or German soil than in the mystical traditions, the catholic conservatism and the harsh political realities of Burgundian history.

He must have come to the Diet with some realisation of the vast and difficult problems which were likely to face him there, for the Lutheran issue was only one among a host of questions which needed to be resolved. The constitution of the Diet, as that of the Empire itself, bore little relation to the needs of the contemporary situation. Several vain attempts had already been made to make the constitution more effective and workable; but so far with only meagre results. A constitution of sorts had indeed been promulgated (which included a clause of some relevance to Luther, declaring that no German should be taken outside Germany for trial or outlawed without due cause and hearing); but what had been so far done was no real answer to the seemingly insoluble problem of how to make the Emperor's authority operative outside his own estates or how to give him the necessary resources in men and money. There was also the question of Imperial relations with the estates of the Diet, with the German princes both great and small, with the bishops, with the free German cities, with the Imperial knights, all the varying congeries of powers split by different interests vertically and horizontally and yet bound together by a vague Teutonic consciousness. The Emperor was not a constitutional monarch but his power was checked and counter-checked by his need for co-operation with the German princes. He could take no final decision without considering how it would affect all interested parties and virtually without their consent. Yet these were only some of the problems with which he had to deal. He had to take precautions for the defence of the eastern frontiers of his dominions against the marauding Turks. He had to take into account the long-term repercussions of his Imperial policies on his other dominions, notably the Low Countries and Spain. He had to devise a programme for containing the

97

French and yet regaining the lost Burgundian lands of which past French kings had deprived his grandmother, Mary of Burgundy. He had to ensure that Imperial (and Spanish) influence was preserved in the Italian peninsula, more especially in the north which formed the virtual life-line between the two most important parts of his dominions. It was essential that he should have the support of the Pope, but equally important that if the Pope supported the Valois kings of France the Pope should be brought to heel. Among his numerous, occasionally exotic and sometimes meaningless, titles, Charles enjoyed that of the King of the Romans, and he hoped eventually to be crowned by the Pope himself. His coronation, which took place at Bologna in 1530, was actually to be the last in the long history of the Empire.

Charles' Italian interests as well as his opposition to the French involved him necessarily in the intricate network of papal politics. Neither Charles nor the Pope could follow a single-minded policy or take a decision that was founded on religious considerations alone without wondering about the subsequent chain reaction. The secular interests of the Papacy, and of the Medici house which supplied two Popes at this time, Leo X and Clement VII, his successor, in particular, made it oppose the extension of Imperial power in Italy. If there had not been these political complications, Charles acting in collaboration with the Pope might have been in a much more advantageous position to deal with the problem presented by Luther and his adherents.

It is doubtful whether Charles himself realised all the possible intricacies when he was brought face to face with a man who seemed to him an obstinate, heretical monk. Although he was in his general policy most concerned with protecting the interests of his family, he was throughout his life a conventionally devout Catholic. Religion meant far more to him than, for instance, it did to his contemporary and rival, Francis I of France. From his earliest youth his life had been saturated in religious observance, and he held the Church in uncritical veneration. He was indeed later to find the behaviour of individual popes profoundly irritating and almost un-Christian; but he did not believe that the low standards of its officials affected the validity of the Church or its sacraments. The papal office in the last resort was unaffected by the personal character of its holder. The Church was a God-given, apostolic instrument for the salvation of men. Charles was a matter of fact man. His morals were not irreproachable, and he was certainly no theologian. In religious affairs he was a cautious conservative. If he had read Luther's works, he would have thought them tiresome, impertinent and revolutionary; the mystical quality of his devotion would

have made little impact on his unimaginative realism. Yet he understood firmly enough that his own authority had been given to him by
God and that it carried with it a definite responsibility. He was by his
office a protector and defender of the Church and of the faith of the
Church. He realised that the Church needed reform, for he had been
brought up in an environment shaped in part by the ideas of the
conciliar movement; but he found the spectacle of a monk challenging
the traditions and authority made sacrosanct by history singularly
hubristic and distasteful. The decision which he was to finally reach at
Worms was one which he felt personally as well as politically to be
correct.

Much intricate negotiation had, however, proved necessary before
the final invitation had been despatched to Luther to appear at Worms.
In August, 1520, Luther had himself appealed to the Emperor: 'It is
not impertinent that one who through the truth of the Gospel has
reached the throne of Divine Majesty should approach the throne of an
earthly prince, nor is it improper that an earthly prince, who is the
image of the Heavenly, should stoop to raise up the poor from the dust.
Consequently, unworthy and poor though I be, I prostrate myself
before your Imperial Majesty. I have published books which have
alienated many, but I have done so because driven by others, for I
would prefer nothing more than to remain in obscurity. For three years
I have sought peace in vain. I have now but one recourse. I appeal to
Caesar. I have no desire to be defended if I am found to be impious or
heretical. One thing I ask, that neither truth nor error be condemned
unheard and unrefuted.' Luther's view of political authority was
conservative and conventional. He believed that the Prince received
his power from God to rule justly, and he appealed to the chief secular
magistrate to vindicate his subject against the churchmen who sought
to condemn him.

Although Luther had already a wide following, his case must have
seemed unimportant by comparison with the other problems which
confronted the Imperial advisers. It was the Elector Frederick of
Saxony who suggested to two of Charles' advisers, Henry of Nassau
and Chièvres, that it might be expedient to give Luther a hearing. As
they wanted to ensure that the Elector would support the Emperor in
the forthcoming diet they suggested to Charles that he should review
Luther's request favourably and on November 27th, 1520, they told
the Elector that Charles had agreed to his bringing Luther to Worms.
This, however, was not what Frederick wanted. He wanted the
Emperor to summon Luther directly. He did not himself wish to be

necessarily identified with Luther's cause or to assume responsibility for him. As Aleander told the Roman curial officials, Luther had many friends at the Saxon court upon whom the Elector placed great reliance. He seems honestly to have admired Luther's courage and tenacity, but he had not embraced his religious views. Luther was for the Elector as well as for the Emperor a hostage in a complex game of German politics. The Elector was desirous of negotiating a marriage between his nephew, John Frederick, and the Emperor's sister, Catherine. He did not wish therefore to suggest that he was too much of a partisan. So he refused to bring Luther to Worms himself. Even before the news of his refusal reached the Imperial court, Charles, perhaps responding to the influence which the papal legate was bringing to bear and returning to his own instinctive reaction, decided to rescind the invitation.

Much to his satisfaction Aleander's influence with the Emperor had grown during the winter of 1520; but he was none the less uneasy at the apparent willingness of Charles' advisers to temporise as by the growing evidence for Luther's own popularity with the ordinary people of Germany. 'Martin', he wrote, 'is depicted with a halo and a dove about his head. The people kiss these pictures. So many have been sold that I was not able to buy one. A cartoon has been appearing portraying Luther with a book in his hand accompanied by Hutten in armour with a sword under the caption "Champions of Christian Liberty". Another sheet shows Luther in front and Hutten behind carrying a chest on which are two chalices with the inscription, "The Ark of the True Faith". Erasmus, in front, is playing the harp as David. In the background is John Hus, whom Luther has recently proclaimed as his saint. In another part of the picture the Pope and the cardinals are being bound by the soldiers of the guard. I cannot go out on the streets but the Germans put their hands to their swords and gnash their teeth at me. I hope the Pope will give me a plenary indulgence and look after my brothers and sisters if anything happens to me.' Thus the papal nuncio prognosticated gloomily in his lodgings, but his influence at court remained considerable.

While Luther waited in Wittenberg, indefatigably industrious, teaching, studying and writing, for he had the unusual knack of being able to concentrate in moments of anxiety on the work in hand, cavalcades of princes and nobles, knights and citizens were moving through the winter's cold towards the city of Worms where the burghers were rubbing their hands at the thought of the profitable business which the Diet would undoubtedly bring to their town.

The price of lodgings and of food rose to unprecedented heights; wine and beer was consumed in vast quantities. A councillor from Nuremberg, Spengler, noticed that many of the leading churchmen spent much of their time, even after Lent had begun, in gambling and feasting; while the presence of so many armed retainers, and of other undesirable disorderly elements, stimulated gangsterdom and robbery. 'Things are here much as they are in Rome', the humanist, Dietrich Butzbach, commented, 'with murder and theft; all the streets are full of prostitutes; there is no Lent here, but jousting, whoring, eating of meat, mutton, pigeons, eggs, milk, and cheese, and there are such doings as in the mountain of Dame Venus.'

The Diet had opened, only three weeks late, with solemn mass in the Cathedral on January 27th, 1521. A copy of Luther's appeal was presented to the Emperor on February 6th, but he tore it up. The gratified papal nuncio picked up the pieces and sent them to Rome. Six days later Aleander was asked to address the Diet, and in a three-hour speech he outlined the familiar arguments against Luther, stressing the fact that he had condemned the findings of the Council of Constance (attempting in this way to win over those who put their trust in the calling of a General Council) and mentioning once again his own discovery of a document which showed that the Greek Emperor, John Paleologus, had accepted the supremacy of the Pope; but he did not himself produce the papal bull excommunicating Luther, thus providing an opportunity for his critics who argued that they were being asked to outlaw a man who had not yet been banned by the Church. The Emperor was persuaded by Aleander's arguments to agree that the edict banning Luther ought to be promulgated if the princes gave their assent. This, however, they failed to do and, if Aleander's account is correct, they became so heated that they started to fight among themselves. On February 19th, 1521, the Estates recommended that Luther should in fact be summoned to attend the Diet, not indeed to engage in equal debate but to answer certain questions put to him by theological experts. If his replies were unsatisfactory, they would agree to the publication of the edict; but they alleged that if Luther was to be condemned without having been given an opportunity to clear himself this would only further inflame public opinion in his favour. Perturbed by this new development, Aleander wrote hastily to Gattinara in the hope that Charles might yet refuse the Estates' request.

It did indeed prove difficult to reach a decision but the Emperor was keen to secure the Estates' support for the publication of the edict and so eventually fell in with their proposal. On March 6th, 1521, a letter was penned to our 'dear, honoured and pious Dr. Martin Luther of the Augustinian Order' requesting him to come to Worms within 21 days 'in order to receive . . . information from him regarding the doctrine and the books which have from time to time come from him', and promising him a safe-conduct, but it was not until March 16th or 17th that the herald of the Empire, Kaspar Sturm, left Worms for Wittenberg, bearing the invitation. The sending of the herald himself was a courteous gesture which showed that the Estates were seriously concerned that Luther should attend the Diet, but it enraged and disconcerted the papal legate. He and his friends were using every possible means to discredit the Saxon monk, suggesting that he was another Hus, and intimating the Pope would more readily bestow benefices on those who toed the papal line. Moreover the Imperial edict against Luther had now been issued, though its immediate effect seems to have been slight; the Nuremberg councillor, Spengler, reported that in some towns the placards were torn down as soon as they were posted and that if anything public opinion was still turning in Luther's favour.

Luther did not long hesitate after the receipt of the Imperial missive, only delaying his departure until the Easter festival had ended. 'I will reply to the Emperor', he had written to Spalatin, 'that if I am being invited simply to recant I will not come. If to recant is all that is wanted, I can do that perfectly well right here. But if he is inviting me to my death, then I will come. I hope none but the papists will stain their hands in my blood. Antichrist reigns. The Lord's will be done.' In spite of such gloomy forebodings, a little cavalcade, consisting of Luther and three companions bearing the 20 gulden granted by the university towards their travelling expenses, at last left Wittenberg.

The journey was uneventful, though it was only after they had started that Luther learned that the edict against him had actually been published. He and his companions beguiled the time with donnish conversation; how far, they discussed for instance, was the book of Joshua a pre-image of the Gospel. At Erfurt, where Luther thought the university officials might show fight, he preached on justification by faith and vigorously scholastic philosophy. He was welcomed at Gotha, Eisenach and Frankfort-on-the-Main. At Oppenheim he was greeted by young Martin Bucer who brought an invitation from von Sickingen and Hutten asking him to join them at the Castle Ebernburg. Whether this was a subtle plan by the Emperor's confessor,

Glapion (who had just had a signal success in persuading the out-spoken Hutten to enter the Imperial service), to prevent Luther's appearance at Worms, at least until the expiry of his safe-conduct, or an attempt by Sickingen who may have doubted whether a safe-conduct given to a heretic would be honoured to ensure Luther's safety seems uncertain; but having gone so far Luther had no wish to retreat. His mood was a queer mixture of depression and elation. The memories of the recent Holy Week were so strongly and strangely impressed on his mind that he could not easily forget the *via dolorosa* of his Lord. After a tumultuous reception at Erfurt he admitted to his friends: 'I have had my Palm Sunday. I wonder whether this pomp is merely a temptation or whether it is also the sign of my impending passion.' To Spalatin he wrote from Frankfort: 'We will enter Worms in spite of all the gates of hell and the powers of the air . . . so make ready the lodgings'.

'The gates of hell and the powers of the air' seemed indeed remark-ably immobile. When he arrived at Worms on the morning of April 16th, 1521, he was accompanied and cheered by a numerous crowd, a fact which Aleander noted with chagrin. A priest had actually bent forward to touch his habit as if he were a saint. As he stepped down from his wagon Luther remarked '*Deus erit pro me*', and all, Aleander wrote blackly, all the world had gone out to him. 'The Elector of Saxony is already ruling and commanding . . . against God and against reason.' Aleander, finding the climate of Worms as lowering as the company, was prone to depression, and he could not foresee how Luther would behave in the unaccustomed environ-ment of the Imperial court.

At the first meeting Luther seemed to have lost something of his accustomed confidence. The procedure had been staged by Aleander and the Emperor's confessor, Glapion, to give Martin as little oppor-tunity as possible. The hereditary marshal, Ulrich von Pappenheim, arrived at four in the afternoon at the house of the Knights of St. John where Luther was lodging to escort him to the Bishop's palace where the Emperor was housed. The Bishop's chamber was naturally crowded beyond its capacity, and was stiflingly hot as the sturdy monk was brought before the Emperor and told that he must only answer the questions put to him. He seemed to a contemporary observer 'a man . . . of forty years of age, more or less, vigorous in expression and physique, eyes without distinction, mobile of countenance and frivolously changing his expression. He wore the habit of the order of St. Augustine, with leather girdle, his tonsure large and recently shaven, his hair close clipped.' Charles' immediate reaction was equally unfavourable. 'This man', he said shortly afterwards, 'will never make me a heretic.' Luther's books had been piled on a nearby bench. The jurist, John von Eck (not to be confused with Luther's opponent of the same name at Leipzig), at once asked Luther, first in Latin and then in German, whether the books attributed to him were in fact his own, and whether he wished to stand by their contents or in any way revoke his opinions. After a lawyer had read out a list Luther replied that he was certainly the author of the books, but he would like further time before he answered the second question inasmuch as it was a matter of faith and the salvation of souls and concerned the Word of God. He spoke so softly that some of the bystanders failed to catch the words, and in general he appeared somewhat nervous and unsure of himself. His friends had patently told him that it would be wiser to play for time. It was very likely that the experience of entering the lions' den itself, of being surrounded by the leading churchmen and nobles of the Empire, in the presence of the secular head of Christendom himself, at first proved unnerving and disconcerting to the academic whose forebears still farmed the

18   Luther's second hearing at Worms
From Bainton, 'Here I Stand', Abingdon Press

19 Emperor Charles V
From a portrait by Jan Cornelisz Vermeyen, c. 1526

Hieronymus Aleander Archiepiscopus brundis
et eius vitam et C nr

20   Cardinal Aleander
From an anonymous drawing

Thuringian lands. Von Eck rebuked Martin for not having realised beforehand that such questions would be put to him, but gave him 24 hours to prepare an oral reply. He spoke at length, using a prepared oration in which he besought Luther not to divide the Church or to disturb the State, laying bare the radical effects of his own personal interpretation of the Scriptures and appealing to him to accept the gracious offers which the Pope and Emperor had given him. Luther might well have felt that the issue was already prejudged and Aleander, who had purposely and wisely absented himself from the proceedings, must have been moderately encouraged by what had so far taken place, though he was doubtless incensed to learn of the shouts of encouragement which reached Luther as he pushed his way through the thronged hall and out into the narrow, crowded streets.

If Luther lacked some of his normal confidence on April 17th, he had regained his self-assurance when he walked the next day towards the Bishop's hall. Because of the discomfort experienced by the spectators during the previous session, a larger chamber had been engaged for the meeting. Even so the room was so packed that Luther had difficulty in making his way to his place. Eck reviewed the proceedings at tiresome length before he reiterated his second question of the previous day. Luther spoke in German 'with becoming modesty and yet with Christian vehemence and forcefulness', making it plain that he had no intention of revoking his opinions. Then, after a hesitant start, for he was uncomfortable and sweating profusely in the hot room, he translated his reply into Latin. 'Truly with the help of Christ I will not revoke even an iota into all eternity.' He readily admitted that his attacks on the Papacy had perhaps been more violent than was becoming to a churchman, 'for I do not set myself up to be a saint, nor do I argue about my life, but about the doctrines of the Christ'. Yet his protest had been called forth by an intolerable situation. The conscience of the Christian world had been held captive too long by canon law and papal policy; the German people are in danger of destruction because of Roman tyranny. He cannot possibly revoke what he holds to be true, though he will listen patiently to any arguments that can be made against his teaching. He is not unlike Christ before the High Priest, and like Christ he is ready to hear the charges against himself. Once more he had made publicly the identification between the sinful Luther and the spotless Christ which threaded his devotional life. 'Testify and point out my errors', he declared (though without the slightest intention of changing his mind). 'Vanquish me with the writings of the prophets and evangelists, for if I shall be thus instructed

I will be most ready to recant any error and will, indeed, be the first to hurl my little books into the flames.' It was a rhetorical statement which held out little promise of genuine conciliation or compromise. He expressed his hopes that the new reign of 'this best young prince Charles', looking impassively and possibly sourly at the performance, would augur well and he bade his lord listen to the Word of God. 'Herewith', he concluded, 'I commend myself to your Majesty and to your governors with the humble prayer that you do not suffer me to be delivered over without cause as a mischievous person to the fanaticism of my adversaries. I have spoken.'

It was a fine performance, controlled, vigorous and firm but free from abuse. It provoked a reply from von Eck, pointing out the 'errors' in Luther's statement. He tried to show that Luther was one in the long line of heretics, claiming, as Arius had so long ago, that his book contained the truth, and putting forward notions which earlier heretics had held and which the Church had rightly condemned. But no man, von Eck argued, can be justified in challenging the authority of Christ's own Church and in asserting his own interpretation of Scripture which the 'most sacred doctors have sought for, sweating day and night', more especially as such activity ultimately only brought profit to Jews and infidels. A single man, so it would seem, had challenged a faith established by Christ, preached by the Apostles, sustained by numerous miracles and confirmed by history. All that can be demanded of Luther is a 'sincere, candid, unambiguous answer, without horns' to the question as to whether Luther will revoke his books and errors or not.

Amidst a tense silence Martin rose and spoke softly. 'If then, Your Majesty and rulers ask for a simple answer, I will give it without horns and without teeth, as follows. Unless I am shown by the testimony of Scripture and by evident reasoning (for I do not put faith in pope or councils alone, because it is established that they have often erred and contradicted themselves), unless I am overcome by means of the scriptural passages that I have cited, and unless my conscience is taken captive by the words of God, I am neither able or willing to revoke anything, since to act against one's conscience is neither safe nor honest.' He then added ' *Gott helf mir, amen* ' which a later rendering transmuted into the more dramatic but no more meaningful words: 'Here I stand; God help me. I cannot do otherwise.'

The monk and his companions passed through the crowd to the street where there were signs of trouble when the rumour spread that soldiers were coming to arrest him. Once he had made his position plain, Luther's spirits rose. As he and his friends left the

Bishop's hall they had 'raised their arms, moving the hands and the fingers, as the Germans do for a signal of victory at the tournament'. When he at last arrived at his lodgings he shouted to the bystanders '*Ich bin hindurch, ich bin hindurch*' ('I've come through, I've come through'). The end was, however, not yet in sight. He had indeed maintained his stand but he had issued a challenge in the presence of the Emperor and the Estates equally to the authority of the Church and the State.

In doing so, he had at least brought the Emperor to a decision. The arguments which von Eck had used confirmed him in his belief that Luther was an arrogant revolutionary and a vulgar showman whose heretical and impertinent opinions had been established beyond doubt. He summoned the Estates to meet him the next morning at eight and then and there read a statement in his native French, which he very probably had drawn up himself at the conclusion of the previous day's meeting. 'I am descended from a long line of Christian Emperors of this noble German nation, and of the Catholic kings of Spain, the archdukes of Austria, and the dukes of Burgundy', he told his intrigued audience, 'They were faithful to the death to the Church of Rome, and they defended the Catholic faith and the honour of God. I have resolved to follow in their footsteps. A single friar who goes counter to all Christianity for a thousand years must be wrong. Therefore I am resolved to stake my lands, my friends, my body, my blood, my life, and my soul. Not only I, but you of this noble German nation would be forever disgraced if by our negligence not only heresy but the very suspicion of heresy were to survive. After having heard yesterday the obstinate defence of Luther, I regret that I have so long delayed in proceedings against him and his false teaching. I will have no more to do with him. He may return under a safe-conduct, but without preaching or making any tumult. I will proceed against him as a notorious heretic, and ask you to declare yourselves as you promised me.'

This was a noble, candid profession of faith, honest and resolute; but it did not produce quite the effect for which the Emperor hoped. Many members of the Estate, who had expected a less rapid and a less positive reaction, turned pale as the Emperor spoke. The papal nuncio could not have been better pleased. But the Estates were not prepared to give up hope of a possible compromise. When the following day the Emperor asked the Electors (who formed the first Estate of the Diet) to approve his action, only four of the six signified their assent, Ludwig of the Palatinate and Frederick of Saxony remaining silent. The division was ominous and was to be repeated at lower levels. Some feared that trouble might break out in the tense, excited atmosphere of the crowded city. The walls were placarded with broadsheets for and against Luther. One bore a threefold '*bundschuh*', a peasant's boot long the symbol of rebellion. The Archbishop of Mainz, one of the Electors and a target of Luther's criticism, perturbed by the evident hostility of the people, advised the Emperor to consent to a new hearing before scholars in the presence of the Electors.

Charles could not disregard the dismay with which his decision had been greeted. On April 20th, 1521, the Estates presented a petition, stating that as Luther had promised that he would be willing to accept a scriptural proof of his errors, a commission of three or four persons 'serious and instructed in the Scriptures' should be appointed to show Luther how his teaching was opposed to the true faith and to the decisions of Church councils. If he was then persuaded of the error of his ways, so much the better; if he still showed himself obdurate, there could be no possible reason for not executing the Imperial edict. If the Estates' proposition was accepted, it would also prove that everything possible had been done to meet the wishes of the friar and his supporters. Although Aleander was worried lest this might be yet another attempt to reach a compromise, Charles eventually agreed to the request, as long as he or his council was not directly involved and as long as Luther did not delay his departure for more than three days.

The Imperial consent given on Monday, April 22nd, 1521, the Estates nominated a commission which met promptly at six the next morning to arrange procedure. Luther was asked to attend at the same hour the following day at the lodgings of Richard von Greiffenklau, the Archbishop of Trier, who had been appointed head of the commission. Its other members included Luther's severe critic, Duke George of Saxony, his ecclesiastical superior, the Bishop of Brandenburg, the Elector Joachim of Brandenburg and the humanist, Peutinger; their spokesman was the fair-minded, clear-headed lawyer, Hieronymus Vehus, the chancellor of the Margrave of Baden. Luther was himself accompanied by Hieronymus Schurf, a Saxon lawyer, Nikolaus von Amsdorf, the theologian and Justus Jonas, the scholarly rector of Erfurt University.

The commission was sincerely concerned to find a way out from the impasse. In his opening speech Vehus emphasised that Christian councils were anxious to establish the truth and were not simply hidebound preservers of past traditions, and he implied, what indeed Aleander feared, that if a General Council was called in Germany it could deal effectively with the evils that Luther had attacked. At the same time he also stressed the dangers that followed the continued circulation of Luther's writings which encouraged the defiance of the law of Church and State. Luther replied that although he condemned the Council of Constance for its unjust treatment of Hus, he did not thereby condemn all councils, but even their decisions stood or fell by the authority of Scripture. He was not indeed defending himself so much as the Word of God. 'I can never make the Lord Christ other than God himself made Him; if we insist on fending off offence and hardship, we then bring them on ourselves in earnest, for the sacred Word of God has always looked as if it were going to cause the earth to collapse and the heavens to fall.' Later in the day the Archbishop called Luther and two of his companions to another room where they had a discussion with the jurist, von Eck, and John Cochlaeus, a former supporter of Luther's who had gone over to his opponents; but the arguments, interminable and sophisticated, led nowhere. After dinner Cochlaeus visited Luther at his lodgings where another conversation took place. Luther was in high spirits, cheerful and friendly, but none of the difficulties were resolved.

In a final effort to prevent the failure of the discussions, Vehus and Peutinger adopted a suggestion put forward by Luther's friend, Schurf, that he should be asked to submit his writings to the Emperor and the Estates with the reservation that 'nothing should be done against evangelical doctrine and God's word'. The Archbishop of Trier obtained a two-days' extension of Luther's safe-conduct and conversations were re-opened. Luther, however, insisted that he would not submit his writings unless it was first agreed by all that the Word of God was free and independent of human judgment. He also made the point justifiably enough that the authority to whom he was asked to submit his books had already in fact condemned them to be burned and had issued an edict against him. Vehus and Peutinger used all their tact and believed that they were gaining ground, so much so that Archbishop Greiffenklau consented to have a private talk with him. He was gracious and Luther was friendly, but the reformer would make no concessions. 'I would rather lose life and head than desert so clearly the Word of God.' He reminded the Archbishop of Gamaliel's comment that if his teaching was of God it would persist; if it were not it would perish within three years.

There could be no real hope of an agreed solution. Luther was granted 21 days within which to return to Wittenberg under safe-conduct, and he was told that he must not preach or otherwise stir up people on his return journey. 'I have never wanted anything', he told the Imperial representative who came to deliver the formal document of dismissal, 'other than a reformation by means of sacred Scripture, and for this I have earnestly striven. For the rest, I would suffer for his Imperial Majesty and the empire all things, life and death, fame and infamy, reserving absolutely nothing for myself except liberty of confessing and testifying freely to the Word of God.'

Martin and his friends sat up late their last night at Worms, drinking Malmsey wine and talking with those who came to bid them farewell. Then on April 26th, 1521, about ten in the morning, Luther and his small cavalcade left the city. The Elector had sent him 40 gulden towards the cost of the journey, but the little group was not in fact to reach Wittenberg. Whether Luther knew this or not at the time seems doubtful, but he must have clearly realised that in his own struggle he had crossed the Rubicon. There could be no turning back now.

CHAPTER 6

Luther and the Progress of the Reformation at Wittenberg

1521–1524

If the Edict of Worms was a victory for the papalists, it was not one which they could put to good use. Lutheranism grew apace during the next three years, slowly beginning to find sympathetic backing from some of the German princes, so much so that when the Imperial Diet met at Nuremberg in 1523, it was face to face with an entirely changed situation. This is perhaps the more surprising as for some months Luther was himself a voluntary exile in the castle of Wartburg, and even on his return he confined his activities to Wittenberg and the surrounding region. The wide sale of his published writings, inflaming his readers against the established Church, tending to exaggerate existing abuses and known corruption, reinforcing inarticulate anti-clerical opinion, in part explains the rapid growth of reformed ideas. 'I perceive', the Emperor's secretary, Valdes, wrote, 'that the minds of the Germans are generally exasperated against the Roman see, and they do not seem to attach great importance to the Emperor's edicts, for since their publication Lutheran books are sold with impunity at every step and corner of the streets and in the market places.' These editions, though small in number, were bought up as soon as they were fresh from the press. Between 1517 and 1520 some 370 editions of his writings appeared, selling, it has been estimated, some 300,000 copies. Indeed the production of Luther's works became so profitable to the printing trade that anti-Lutheran writers often found it difficult to obtain a publisher, and Luther himself found it necessary to inveigh against the circulation of pirated and unauthorised editions of his writings, which he did with his normal verve.

There were other factors which contributed to the remarkable expansion of Lutheranism in this period. As yet the greater princes remained somewhat aloof, hardly fully aware of the extent to which Luther's teaching could be employed to further their own territorial and constitutional advantages. Luther had, however, a rising reputation as a theologian who had created a school at Wittenberg which attracted the attention of the young aspirant to academic honours. If there was a drop in the numbers enrolled following his condemnation, some 16,292 students entered the university between 1520 and 1560, the majority from German-speaking lands. His teaching, refreshingly direct, defiant of the long-dominant scholasticism, seemed to make him a representative of the theological *avant-garde* of his time; few of the 'angry young men' who read his works or flocked to his lectures realised the basic conservatism of his position. He had colleagues like Carlstadt and Melanchthon, followers like Bucer and others who never achieved eminence but who contributed to disseminate his views through the churches. If the bulk of the support for the German reformation came from the laity, the lead was certainly taken by the churchmen. Although Luther was opposed to the notion, a Lutheran party, to some extent stocked by graduates from Wittenberg, had come into being and was enthusiastically engaged in spreading his ideas.

Moreover the time had arrived when his ideas found a practical manifestation, which must have done more than anything else to bring the theologically indifferent an indication of the things for which Luther seemed to stand. What was happening at Wittenberg, the rejection of the Mass, the closing of the monasteries and so forth, was soon to be repeated all over Germany. Doubtless there was a religious need which Luther's teaching certainly met; but there was more than religious ingredients in the development of the Reformation. The physical pleasure which acts of violence and destruction stimulate may well have had its part in attracting some of the young men to his standard; when they entered the parish church at Wittenberg to drive out the priests and seize the mass books they concealed daggers under their cloaks. There was perhaps less concern for freedom for the Gospel than freedom from the Pope. Luther had supplied a dynamic which tumbled the old gods from the altar, ended age-old ecclesiastical demands and broke the spell which canon law, scholastic theology and sacramental sanctions had established over the Church. Monks and nuns who had embraced life-long vows of chastity, poverty and obedience when they were impressionable adolescents, or even earlier, found that they had been deceived into thinking that their obligations were scriptural. Marriage, Luther explained, was not merely physically enjoyable but spiritually commendable. The supporters of the established order were correct in supposing that Luther's teaching sabotaged the authority of the Church, and that the control which the sacerdotal order had in its own interests exercised over the laity had been effectively challenged. Neither they nor Luther were aware of the full implications of the reformed teaching. Indeed Luther himself began to be worried by the radicalism of some of his followers.

The potential social dangers which Lutheranism fostered were displayed, so some of his critics alleged, in the armed attack which Franz von Sickingen and his knights made on the estates of the Archbishop-Elector of Trier in 1522. Von Sickingen represented a class of knights whose fortunes had been sadly depleted both by the better maintenance of law and order in Germany and by economic developments. In a desperate attempt to retrieve his influence and wealth he led an armed rising which ended in a disastrous defeat and his own death at Landstuhl in the spring of 1523. Neither von Sickingen nor his humanist soldier friend, the poet Ulrich von Hutten, acted under the aegis of or with the approval of Luther; but they were both associated with criticisms of the contemporary Church and attacks on its property. Hutten was a shrill, vehement critic of the corruption of the Church and he found fuel in Luther's writings for his own fulminations. Luther was no doubt gratified by the friendly attitude of Sickingen and Hutten, for on the eve of the Diet of Worms any such sympathy was warmly welcome. He refused Sickingen's invitation to stay at the Ebernburg, but he rather sycophantically dedicated a tract to the knightly adventurer in language which seems to the distant observer strangely inapposite. He did not, however, approve of the violence they were advocating and he disowned Sickingen's attack on Church lands. Sickingen was, however, as dead as the cause he represented; while Hutten, diseased and desperate, found a little refuge on the little island of Ufenau among the reeds of the lake of Zürich where, befriended by Zwingli, he died in 1523. Although Luther's connection with the Knights' War was tenuous indeed, hostile critics necessarily associated the policy of violence with his teaching, of which Hutten was a self-acclaimed herald.

By 1524 Luther had raised a whirlwind; his writings were read in Cambridge and London as well as in Paris and Brussels. He had become a European as well as German figure. But what of the man himself in these years? He had set out from Worms that spring morning in 1521 with the intention of returning to Wittenberg but shortly before he reached Eisenach, armed horsemen had appeared who escorted the reformer to the medieval fortress of the Wartburg. The Elector Frederick had himself agreed to the scheme for kidnapping Luther, in part to protect him from his adversaries who wished to put the Edict of Worms into operation and in part to keep a watchful eye and a restraining hand on his pugnacious subject, for the Elector's own position was in some respects delicate. The outside world soon buzzed with rumours as to Luther's fate. Some said that he had been seized by agents of Aleander or of the Archbishop of Mainz, others, by the Franconian knights, others, that his body had actually been discovered in a silver mine with a dagger plunged through it. 'O God', exclaimed Albrecht Dürer when this supposed news reached him in the Low Countries, 'if Luther is dead who will henceforth expound the holy Gospel so clearly to us?' Luther was, however, very much alive. He had discarded his friar's habit, dressed as a layman, let his beard and tonsure grow; he became known to the inhabitants of his neighbourhood as Junker George. Bucer writing to Zwingli on May 23rd, 1521, 19 days after his arrival at the castle, hit the nail on the head when he said: 'You may take it from me that Luther has indeed been taken captive, but unless I am very much mistaken, not at all by his enemies. The affair has been admirably screened and very discreetly carried out.'

Luther was himself less sure. Life in a monastery had already disclosed that he was not ideally suited to a contemplative existence. He would personally have preferred to have been in the thick of the fight, not vegetating in comfort in a gaunt castle, waited on by two pages, his identity known only to the warden, Hans von Berlepsch, and his immediate attendants. 'Here I sit an odd capture, willing and yet unwilling—willing because God so wills it, unwilling because I should prefer to stand forth in behalf of the Word, but have not yet been found worthy.' 'I sit here inactive and out of sorts the whole day long', he wrote to Spalatin on May 14th, 1521. The good food and the lack of physical exercise again brought on constipation, and as its sequel piles, from which he suffered at Worms. He was beset by insomnia, and when he eventually slept he was the victim of nightmares. The Devil was everywhere. He heard him rattling the hazel nuts in a sack; he listened to him scuttling down the stairs, making a great racket of it as his cloven hoofs hit the stone. He appeared as a black dog, laying on Luther's bed until he threw it out of the window: 'I can tell you in this idle solitude there are a thousand battles with Satan.' He felt depressed and lonely, so much so that he thought of leaving his eyrie to seek medical advice at Erfurt. He was evidently experiencing an acute reaction from the emotional and intellectual crisis through which he had passed during his stay at Worms. He may well have had feelings of guilt as he considered the implications of the movement which he had set in train; but equally he felt a sense of inadequacy as he confronted the trials which lay in front of him. 'For the last eight days', he told Melanchthon on July 13th, 1521, 'I have written nothing. I neither pray nor study, partly on account of the trials of the flesh, partly because I am tormented with another malady. If my condition does not improve, I shall throw off this disguise and go to Erfurt to consult the doctors, and you will see me there. For I can bear this wretchedness no longer. Nay, I would suffer ten serious wounds more easily than this one seemingly slight lesion. Perchance the Lord thus torments me that He may force me out of this hermitage into the public arena.' The Warden took him hunting in the hope that this would divert him, but Luther's sensitive spirit was bruised by man's inhumanity, an unusual trait in his age. 'There is some point in tracking down bears, wolves and foxes, but why should one pursue a harmless creature like a rabbit?', he wrote. A hare took refuge in his sleeve and, to Luther's disgust, the dogs bit through it to their prey. Even amidst the excitement of the hunt, he found an analogue to his own experience. 'So rage the Pope and Satan in order to destroy the souls I have saved, caring nothing for my efforts to rescue them.'

Biblia: das ist:
Die gantze Heilige
Schrifft: Deudsch
Auffs New zugericht.

D. Mart. Luth.

Begnadet mit Kur-
fürstlicher zu Sachsen Freiheit.

Gedruckt zu Wittem-
berg / Durch Hans Lufft.

M·D·XLI·

21   The title-page of Luther's Bible, 1541
From Bainton, 'Here I Stand', Abingdon Press

He called himself 'most inactive' (*otiosissimus*) but he was far from lazy. In some respect he was also 'most busy' (*negotiotissimus*), utilising every moment of his spare time for study and writing. This at least afforded him some relaxation from the menace of depression. 'I have brought out a reply to Catharinus and another to Latomus, and in German a work on confession, expositions of Psalms 67 and 36, a commentary on the *Magnificat*, and a translation of Melanchthon's reply to the University of Paris. I have under way a volume of sermons on the lessons from the Epistles and Gospels. I am attacking the Cardinal of Mainz and expounding the ten lepers.' If his polemic writings were as vigorous and as crude as ever, he had developed a singular gift for expounding the Bible simply and lucidly, making it relevant and intelligible to the common reader. He was working throughout his stay at the Wartburg on a translation of the New Testament into German, a task which Melanchthon had encouraged him to undertake. He used Erasmus' text and worked to such good effect that he had completed the New Testament by the end of February 1522. He approached the problem of translation from the standpoint of the true scholar, using his linguistic ability to convey the true meaning of the text. The original languages in which the Bible was written form 'the sheath in which the sword of the Spirit is encased'. He employed contemporary lexicons and commentaries to aid him in his task: Reuchlin's *Rudimenta Linguae Hebraicae* (1506), Lefèvre's *Psalterium Quincuplex* (1509) and *Epistoli Pauli Apostoli* (1512), Reuchlin's *Septem Psalmi Poenitentiales* (1512) and Melanchthon's *Greek Grammar* (1518) among others. In his treatment of the text he showed an unusual critical power, more especially with regard to the relative value of the different books of the New Testament. 'I long', he wrote, 'that every town should have its own interpreter, and that the tongue, hand, eyes, ears, and hearts of all should be occupied with this book alone.' He was unable to finish his translation of the Old Testament, in part because his library of Hebrew books was inadequate at the Wartburg, but he expressed the hope that he would soon be back at Wittenberg so that he might work quietly at this task.

Even this, however, does not comprise all that engaged him in his exile. He composed devotional works, and he maintained a vast correspondence with friends and others all over Germany, more especially, as was natural, with his colleagues at Wittenberg. Far from being the headquarters of a recluse in exile, the castle had become the nerve-centre of the Reformation. If Luther felt low-spirited, it was in part because of frustration, because at so critical a time he was debarred

119

from taking an active part in the exciting events that were then transforming the religious life of this small and rather dreary township.

Wittenberg had become the scene of radical religious change. It was here that Luther's theological assumptions began to his delight to find practical manifestation in the life of the community. While he was away the lead had been taken by Melanchthon, one of the most attractive of the reformers and by inclination and conviction a scholarly moderate, by Carlstadt, a university professor but much more radically-minded and Gabriel Zwilling, an Augustinian friar and something of a demagogue. Melanchthon in fact found that it was increasingly difficult to restrain his two enthusiastic colleagues. A chapter meeting of the Augustinians, or rather of those friars favourable to Luther's teaching, which had been held at Wittenberg in January, 1522, decided that all members of the order were free if they wished to renounce their vows. Within a few months the prior was the only remaining occupant of the monastery. The former friars, doubtless encouraged by the gift of 100 gulden to repudiate their vows, soon abandoned their vow of chastity, in some cases marrying former nuns, to the scandal of the more conservative-minded. Luther had himself declared earlier that since marriage had been ordained by God, the marriage of a priest under divine law was a valid and indissoluble union. One of his former students, Bernhardi, now provost of Kemsberg in the diocese of Mainz, and two priests in the dioceses of Magdeburg and Meissen, had recently followed his advice; but the two priests had been gaoled by their bishops and the Archbishop of Mainz had called on the Elector (in whose territory Bernhardi lived) to hand over the first culprit. The Elector referred the matter to Melanchthon and his fellow professors at Wittenberg; they urged that the marriage of priests was legitimate since it accorded with the teaching of the Bible and the actual practice of the early Church. Carlstadt took the argument further, declaring that monks and nuns should be everywhere free to marry, and that priests ought to marry and rear a family; he soon followed his own advice by marrying Anna Mochau. In spite of what he had written Luther was not a little embarrassed at the attacks on monastic celibacy and the zest with which the clergy embraced marriage. He had not yet outgrown the training and teaching of earlier years. 'Good God!', he commented to Spalatin, 'our Wittenbergers will give wives even to the monks! But they will not thrust a wife on me!' yet on deeper consideration he could not withhold his approval. Within a few months of Luther's departure from Worms, the cloisters at Wittenberg were virtually empty.

Wie gar gfarlich sey. So
Ain Prieſter kaln Ee weyb hat. Wye Vn
chriſtlich. vnd ſchedlich aim gmainen
Nutz Die menſchen ſeynd. Welche
hindern die Pfaffen Am Ee=
lichen ſtand. Durch
Johan Eberlin Von Güntzburg. Anno.

1522,

22   The marriage of bishops, monks and nuns, 1522
From Bainton, 'Here I Stand', Abingdon Press

Nor was this all. His teaching had become increasingly critical of the contemporary doctrine of the Mass. The stress which he laid on justification by faith challenged its sacrificial aspect. The Mass cannot be regarded as a sacrifice nor even as an oblation since God needs neither to be placated nor offered anything; it is He who gives and men who receive. The Mass must be regarded therefore as a thanksgiving to God for what He has achieved for men through the sacrifice of Christ and a communion of those who believe. The vested interests of the clergy were responsible for the corrupt interpretation placed on it. He more especially condemned the celebration of private masses for the souls of the departed, which seemed to him to contradict the necessary sovereignty of God and the inadequacy of all human works. On what actually happened at the consecration he was neither then or later perfectly clear. He held that the current doctrine of transubstantiation by which the 'accidents' of the bread and wine remained while the substance was changed into the body and blood of Christ was an unjustified invention of the scholastic philosophers; but he none the less held fast to the belief that Christ was really and truly present in the Eucharist.

As in so much else the practice of the apostolic Church, as he understood it, provided the true criterion for judgment. He wished to follow its example by giving communion in two kinds, that is the bread and the wine, instead of the one kind (the bread alone) as had long been the practice in the medieval Church, to the laity. On Michaelmas Day, 1521, Melanchthon gave communion in both kinds to some of the students. Gabriel Zwilling urged a reform of the Mass in the monastery church. On All Saints' Day, 1521, Jonas preached a fierce sermon against indulgences and called for the abolition of vigils and private masses. On the other hand there were ugly scenes in which the students and townsfolk took part not wholly free from intimidation. The zealots—and perhaps some who simply enjoyed the experience— threw stones at those who were saying their devotions to the Virgin.

The news of these revolutionary happenings reaching Luther and his master, the Elector of Saxony, produced rather different reactions. The Elector, who had his political position to consider and did not wish to alienate either the Emperor or his fellow princes, was alarmed by the violent character of the changes, and possibly embarrassed by the sermon which Jonas had preached in the Castle Church in the midst of his own prize collection of relics. Luther was thrilled by what had occurred and was annoyed to learn that three of his outspoken tracts, *On Monastic Vows*, *On the Abolition of Private Masses* and *A Blast*

23   Philip Melanchthon
From an engraving by Albrecht Dürer, c. 1526

24   George Spalatin,
Chaplain to Frederick the Wise
*From a portrait by Lucas
Cranach the Elder*

25   Ulrich Zwingli
*From a portrait by or after
Hans Asper*

Against the Archbishop of Mainz, which he had sent to Spalatin for publication had so far been withheld from the press. He decided to leave his 'island of Patmos', as he sometimes referred to his retreat, to pay a short visit to Wittenberg where, discreetly bearded, he arrived on December 4th, 1521.

His visit served both to encourage and to alarm him. He welcomed the changes which had already been made in the religious life of the town as an evident improvement, and he rejoiced that evangelical teaching affected not merely the monks and the clergy but the lay people of the town. He was worried, however, by what seemed to be the hesitant policy of the Elector. He stoutly criticised the continued existence of the collection of relics in the Castle Church and he recommended that the valuable caskets in which they were stored should be given to a fund to help the poor. He thought too that Spalatin had been insufficiently firm with his master and persuaded him to release for publication his tracts on monastic vows and private masses; though the blast against the Archbishop of Mainz did not materialise. On the other hand his cautious, conservative spirit was perturbed by the undercurrent of violence which had attended the change. 'Remember', he warned his colleagues, 'that Antichrist, as Daniel said, is to be broken without the hand of man. Violence will only make him stronger. Preach, pray, but do not fight. Not that all compulsion is ruled out, but it must be exercised by the established authorities.' Throughout his life he retained his sense of order as divinely sustained and his fear of social revolution as set in train by satanic forces. Although he had been encouraged by the course of events, he returned to Wartburg Castle with some foreboding.

In the event his fears were justified. Under the radical stimulus of Carlstadt and Zwilling the Reformation in Wittenberg gathered impetus at an alarming rate. It was all very well for Luther to advise restraint, but his pen did not especially encourage moderation and temperance and he could hardly blame his followers if they took his denunciation of abuses at its face value. On December 19th, 1521, the Elector, still embarrassed by the news from Wittenberg, ordered that no further changes should be made in the Mass without unanimous approval. In spite of this, Carlstadt declared in a sermon when he preached at All Saints' Church that he none the less intended to administer communion in both kinds on New Year's Day; and on Christmas Eve, fearful that the Elector might intervene if he gave longer warning, he promised that he would put his intention into practice the very next day. The excited Wittenbergers, among them a powerful student element, celebrated the eve of the festival by smashing images and votive lamps, by chanting 'My maid has lost her shoe' in the parish church and by heckling the priests and choir. The following day Carlstadt, habited in a black gown and without the normal vestments, recited the Mass in Latin but in abbreviated form, omitting the all-important passages commemorating the sacrifice and the elevation of the elements at the consecration; furthermore he invited the people in German to take the bread and the wine from the altar with their own hands. In his sermon he stated that fasting and confession were unnecessary for a truly Christian reception of the sacrament. All that God required of the Christian was sincere contrition and a genuine faith. 'See how Christ makes you a sharer in his blessedness if you believe.' These innovations were repeated many times in the following weeks and were confirmed by the town council at its meetings on January 24th–25th, 1522. In addition to approving the administration of communion in two kinds and the liturgical changes which Carlstadt had introduced into the service, the council ordered all the altars, with three exceptions, to be removed from the parish church to avoid idolatry. Church revenues and plate were sequestrated to form a common fund which was to be administered for the benefit of the poor. Monks and friars were forbidden to beg and ordered to work. The income of the various religious fraternities was consolidated into a common fund from which loans could be made to poor workers and the unemployed and money set aside to support orphans and poor children. All images were removed from the churches. Prostitution was banned.

The Wittenbergers seemed to have enjoyed the work of 'reformation'. The former Augustinian friars under Zwilling's lead thrust out the altars from the monastery's chapels, burned the pictures of the saints and smashed the images. In his iconoclastic zeal Carlstadt would have treated organs, trumpets and church music in similar fashion. The rowdy element eagerly followed the reformer's lead. Moreover another ingredient had been added to the existing religious and social ferment through the arrival in Wittenberg of three enthusiastic laymen, Stübner, Storch and Drechsel, disciples of the radical prophet, Thomas Münzer, who had been recently expelled from the neighbouring village of Zwickau for creating disturbances there. Münzer and his followers were visionaries who believed that they were under the direct inspiration of the Holy Spirit, indeed in such close contact that they did not even need the Scriptures to mediate the Word of God. Their ecstatic, woolly teaching, individualistic and antinomian, with powerful undertones of febrile social revolution, added greatly to the general turmoil. Melanchthon, anxious but impressed, wrote favourably to the Elector who can hardly have been pleased to learn of the way in which the reformation was progressing in his favoured university. Luther's innate conservatism made him highly sceptical of the claims made by the prophets of Zwickau: 'Those who are expert in spiritual things have gone through the valley of the shadow. . . . Prove the spirits, and if you are not able to do so, then take the advice of Gamaliel and wait.'

Whether the Saxon Elector was even prepared to go that far was doubtful, nor is it altogether strange that he should have regarded the course of events at Wittenberg with increasing alarm. The canons of All Saints, intimidated by their fellow townsfolk, grumbled bitterly of the insults to themselves and the Catholic faith which they had to endure. The Imperial Estates meeting at Nuremberg were persuaded by Duke George of Saxony to complain of the unjustified innovation in religion that had been made in Wittenberg and its neighbourhood. The Bishop of Meissen on the initiative of the Estates asked permission from the Elector to conduct a visitation of his diocese. In poor health, nervous of the reaction which religious changes in his territory had provoked in Germany, and yet unwilling to disown Luther and his colleagues whose religious sincerity and academic reputation he admired, the Elector faced a dilemma which he could not easily resolve. But on February 13th, he wrote to the Wittenberg authorities and the chapter of the Castle Church: 'We have gone too quickly. . . . The common man has been incited to folly, and no one has been edified. We should have consideration for the weak. Images should be left until further notice. . . . The question of begging should be discussed further. No essential portion of the Mass should be omitted. . . . Carlstadt should not preach any more.'

The town council at Wittenberg could not ignore the Elector's instructions when they were put in such a definitive way. Carlstadt agreed for the moment to suspend his preaching and Zwilling left Wittenberg. But if the Wittenbergers had no wish to quarrel with their ruler and patron, they did not wish to suspend the reformation of the Church. They decided that the most satisfactory way of solving their problems was to invite Luther to return to Wittenberg; he was their original leader and was besides known to be much more in the Elector's confidence than his colleagues. When Frederick heard of the proposed invitation, he was conciliatory, stressed the difficulties of his position, and the confused state of affairs in Wittenberg, urged Luther to curb his impatience and implied that if he did return, he must not necessarily expect the Elector to protect him from the wrath of the Emperor or the Diet. Luther replied firmly that he too had been much concerned at the news from Wittenberg: 'I was worried that the gospel had been brought into discredit at Wittenberg.' He could not doubt that Satan had been at work there, but he was not in favour of making concessions to his critics, for these would only bring the reforms 'into contempt'. He had no doubt whatsoever that he was teaching the Word of God and that the reforms which had been introduced were in some sense divinely inspired. He had only gone into concealment because the Elector had requested it, certainly not from cowardice or choice. He once again displayed his confident faith and prophetic pride by declaring: 'I would have you know that I come to Wittenberg with a higher protection than that of your Grace.' Indeed, he asserted even more sublimely that he, Luther, was probably able to give more protection to the Elector than the latter could provide for him. He was afraid that Frederick was 'weak in the faith. You ask what you should do, and think you have done too little. . . . If your Grace had eyes, you would see the glory of God.' The Elector may well have been impressed by Luther's resolute tone; yet ultimately Luther's life and freedom still depended on his goodwill.

Luther's return to Wittenberg gave a measure of stability to the Reformation there. Two days after his return, March 8th, 1522, he began a series of sermons in the parish church in the course of which he went some way towards adapting the contemporary situation to his theology. If, he declared, we agree that faith is the basic necessary ingredient in the life of the Christian, faith has always to be associated with the law of love. This in its turn requires a display of patience and self-denial. No one can properly deny that what has been done so far to reform the Church has been excellent, but the spirit behind the reforms has been questionable. It has too often contravened the law of love and followed after violence. All real changes require persuasive testimony rather than force. Sow the Word of God, he told his congregation, and leave the rest to God. 'I will preach the Word, will declare it, will write it. But I will never force or press anyone with violence, for faith can only be willingly, unconstrainedly nourished. . . . I have done nothing; the Word everything. If I had so wished, I might have deluged Germany with blood; yea, I might have started such a game at Worms that the Emperor himself would not have been secure. I have only let the Word act.' Clearly his prophetic vocation had been greatly strengthened during his time at Wartburg Castle. His confidence was such that he might seem to be the Word himself.

Yet, by contrast with Carlstadt and some of the more revolutionary preachers, his policy was restrained and moderate. He had no doubt that the changes that had been made in the Mass were theologically correct, but they should have been put into effect more slowly and only with the previous consent of the Elector. There were other matters where reform was abundantly justified, such as celibacy, monasticism, fasting, images and sacred pictures, but where the eventual decision was best left to the conscience of the individual believer. Luther's criticisms may well have betrayed that he was jealous of Carlstadt's enthusiasm; he had the prophet's dislike of able rivals. The ordinances which the town council had passed the previous January were therefore modified to allow a partial restoration of the Latin Mass (though private masses remained under the ban and the sacrificial elements of the Mass were omitted) as of sacred pictures and images. Communion in both kinds was permitted to those who wished to receive in that way but was not made obligatory. The prophets from Zwickau were sent packing: 'See to it', he urged the reformer, Hausmann, at Zwickau, 'that you allow no innovations to be made by public decree and oppressive methods. By the Word alone these images are to be assaulted and overthrown, which our people at Wittenberg have attempted to do by force and violence.' In general Luther's policy met with warm approval. Melanchthon sighed with relief. The Elector must have been equally pleased. Only Carlstadt remained grimly silent, the more irritated by Luther's confiscation of the tract which he had written recently against the papalist, Dungersheim von Ochsenfurt, which contained implied criticisms of the reformer as well.

Yet it is doubtful whether the existing situation could long continue. The canons of the Castle Church held fast to the old order and still sang masses for the departed. Luther felt that the continuance of the old religion in the midst of reformed Wittenberg was a slur on the true Word; the church constituted a 'Bethavum', a 'house of sin', a living reproach to the Gospel. Oblivious of the advice that he had given to the citizens in his preaching a few weeks earlier, he suggested that the Elector should use the revenues of the Castle Church to foster the Gospel and presumably to oust the canons. By the New Year, 1523, he had become convinced that the continued activities of the Church constituted a scandal which prevented the progress of the Gospel and ought no longer to be tolerated. The masses should be brought to an end, the relics dispersed and the revenues of the church confiscated for better purposes. Christians, he declared, are under no obligation to tolerate the obviously scandalous, what constitutes, as he described it

129

in a strangely inappropriate but strong phrase, spiritual fornication. At last, somewhat reluctantly, towards the end of 1524, Frederick gave in to Luther's requests. In the intervening period, the canons, indulgently described by Luther as 'three or four pigs and belly-sowers', had had to endure the stimulated hostility of the townspeople who smashed the Dean's windows and made life so uncomfortable for him that the unfortunate man was at last obliged to write to the Elector to say that it was really impossible to perform the Mass. In this way Luther forced the Elector's hand. The Dean and the Prior vacated the monastic buildings which the Elector, perhaps with a certain irony, presented to Luther together with the garden as his own residence. In truth the cuckoo had won the nest.

Meanwhile reform had been going ahead in other directions. Luther told Spalatin at the beginning of 1523 that he felt that he had been too indulgent towards weak brethren. In March he introduced services of a more distinctively evangelical character in the parish church. He wanted to find a medium for an exposition of the whole of the New and Old Testament, together with prayer and praise; but he was desirous of ensuring that such services should not last longer than an hour, so that the congregation might not be wearied with protracted devotions, the asses' work (*eselarbeit*) so long familiar to Luther through the round of monastic hours. He was equally concerned that the preaching of the Word should become a prominent part of every Sunday service, including the Mass. The celebration of saints' days, except those in honour of the Blessed Virgin, was brought to an end. The actual liturgy of the Mass, with which Carlstadt had previously tinkered, was remoulded in a *formula missae* which he completed in 1523 for use at Wittenberg and other reformed churches. After stating that the priesthood had distorted the celebration of the Lord's Supper which had been instituted by Christ for its own ends, he eliminated the central act in the Mass by which the elements are transmuted by the words of consecration into the body and blood of Christ and in their places substituted the words of institution; he provided for communion in both kinds by priest and people. Henceforth communion in the one kind was disallowed. He recommended the use of hymns in the vernacular. With regard to the other services he was in the main content to translate them into German.

It was impossible to reform the liturgy without transforming the Church which provided the priesthood through which it was mediated to the people. For Luther the Church was the *communio sanctorum*, the gathered community of all those who had been accepted by Christ as His people. 'The being, life and nature of the Christian people is not a bodily assembly together but an assembling together of hearts in one faith.' The ecclesia is the 'Christian holy people in which Christ lives, works and reigns "*per redemptionem*" through grace and forgiveness of sins, and the Holy Ghost "*per vivificationem et sanctificationem*" through the daily purging out of sins and the renewal of its life'. It is God's chosen people, *Gottes Volk.* 'For the Church is and can be nothing else but a congregation of spiritual men, gathered together not into any one particular place, but into the same faith, hope and love of the Spirit . . . the Church of Christ is nothing other than an assembly of spiritual and believing men collected together, in whatsoever part of the world they may be: and whatever of flesh and blood they may be; and knowing also that of whatever person, place, time they may be, and whatsoever things they may have which flesh and blood use, these things pertain not to the Church.' 'I believe that there is on earth, through the whole wide world, no more than one holy, common Christian Church, which is nothing else than the congregation [*Gemeine*] or assembly of the saints, i.e. the good, believing men on earth, which is gathered, preserved, ruled by the Holy Ghost and is daily increased by means of the Sacraments and the Word of God.'

But if the Church is ultimately an invisible society of believers '*coram Deo*', it must find an outward expression in the world. 'The Church must appear in the world. But it can only appear in a covering [*larva*], a veil, a shell, or some kind of clothes which a man can grasp, otherwise it can never be found. But such a mask is a married man, somebody in political or domestic life, John, Peter, Martin, Amsdorf &c yet none of them is the Church, which is neither man nor wife, Jew nor Greek, but Christ alone.' Inspired by a desire to return to the practice of the apostolic Church, he had already slashed at the roots of ecclesiastical order and authority. The Pope appeared to him so much the antithesis of Christ that he could think of him as no less than Antichrist. His hatred had become so intense that no words or phraseology were too obscene to smear the papal curia: 'The only portion of the human anatomy which the Pope has had to leave uncontrolled is the hind end.'

There is fundamentally one Christian estate (*Stand*), but within it the Christians themselves may be called to different offices (*Amt*). All true Christians must be priests with the same right as their fellows to preach the Gospel, to edify and correct their brethren without the virtue of specific ordination. 'Thus it follows that there is really no difference between laymen and priests, princes or bishops, spiritual and temporal, except that of office and work, but not of estate: for they are all Christians, true priests, bishops or popes, though they are not all engaged in the same work.' What Stephen, Philip and others had practised in the apostolic Church, the Christian was equally entitled to do in the sixteenth century. 'Christ has so operated in us that we are able spiritually to act and pray on behalf of one another, just as the priest acts and prays bodily on behalf of the people.' Luther was able to combine his belief in the priesthood of all believers with the existence of a called and consecrated ministry. 'Let everyone therefore who knows himself to be a Christian be assured of this, and apply it to himself that we are all priests and there is no difference between us: that is to say, we have the same power in respect to the Word and Sacraments. However, no one may make use of this power except by consent of the community or the call of the superior. For what is the common property of all, no individual may arrogate to himself, unless he be called.' Although Luther had admitted the need for a ministry, he had none the less challenged the accepted view of the Christian priesthood, more especially its mediatorial function.

It followed that the Christian community or congregation (*Gemeine*) must be theoretically the ultimate authority in ecclesiastical matters in so far as it adhered to the Word of God, for the 'Church does not make the Word of God, but she is made by the Word of God'. The congregation is the embryonic Church, *Kirche im Werden*, not assured that it is *the* Church but constant in its pursuit of its calling and protected by God's grace. 'For while the Word of God flourishes, all things flourish and go well in the Church—and that is the reason that at this day the Church is not only withered away into luxury and pomp but is almost wholly destroyed. It is because the Word of God is disregarded, and the laws of men and the artful inventions of Rome are taught.' In practice, however, the Christian community would seem the administrative unit in religious matters. 'The Christian congregation', he laid down in the rules which he drew up for the church of Leisnig in 1523, 'or community has the right and power to judge of doctrine and appoint and depose its teachers'. 'It can only be constituted and ruled by the divine Word.' All this implied that bishops, already discredited by their worldliness, the canon law, the ministry of the sacraments were only effectively valid if their function was confirmed by the authority of the Word of God.

The village of Leisnig drew up a series of interesting regulations which were founded on the view that the congregation was the divinely constituted authority in these matters. All church property was to be invested in a common fund to support the clergy, the poor, schools and so forth. It is doubtful whether Luther fully realised the implications of his teaching. Indeed although he continued to cherish the notion of the priesthood of believers and of the authority of the congregation, he found that in practice the behaviour of the believers could be disconcerting, even revolutionary; Luther was too confident of his authoritative powers of interpretation to permit the congregation to offer alternative expositions.

Wittenberg afforded an example to the rest of Germany. In the early summer of 1523 Luther himself visited a number of Saxon towns, among them Borna, Zwickau, Eilenburg, Torgau and Altenburg. The town council of the last named requested Luther to nominate a preacher for the parish church. Luther recommended Zwilling, but the provost and chapter of the church of Our Lady on the Mount protested vehemently, claiming the right of appointment. Luther encouraged the Elector to support the town council, alleging that those who, like the chapter, opposed the Word of God automatically forfeited their rights. The Elector eventually agreed to nominate the former Vicar-General of the Augustinians, Link, who at once introduced communion in two kinds. At Erfurt the reformers and their opponents were represented by the former Augustinian prior, Lang, who had only recently renounced his office, and Luther's old teacher, Usingen, whom he now denounced as Usinnen or Herr Nonsense. Here too the reformers sponsored violent and revolutionary methods to obtain power. Luther's own personal evangelism was largely confined to Saxony. Elsewhere his influence made its impact through his immense correspondence, his books and the increasing number of his pupils and followers. 'He', Mackinnon wrote, 'addresses missive after missive to individuals, to churches, to town councils, or other governing bodies. He takes the lead in constituting churches on an evangelical basis and instituting a reformed order of worship. He responds to constant appeals for help and advice and befriends the refugees from the monasteries or the ranks of the secular clergy who flock to Wittenberg, and for whom he strives to find maintenance and a vocation. He provides evangelical preachers for the churches that apply to him from far and near. He appeals to the civil authorities or to the Elector and other magnates on behalf of presecuted brethren and writes letters of comfort and encouragement to the communities in Germany and the Netherlands which are suffering for the faith. Through Spalatin he constantly strives to influence the Elector to adopt a more energetic

policy on behalf of the Gospel, whilst disclaiming any desire to compromise him in his cause with the Emperor and the Regency.'

If Luther was the field-marshal of the Protestant Reformation, he
had to place reliance on his generals and lieutenants. Although
Luther was gifted with an almost unique power for communicating
his thoughts in simple, moving German, the movement which he
headed was fundamentally an intellectual protest. Its earliest leaders
were thus neither demagogues or visionaries, but highly-educated
men, professors and lecturers who held influential posts at German and
Swiss universities. Melanchthon, Luther's colleague as professor of
Greek at Wittenberg, was a judicious scholar whose *Loci Communes*
published at the end of 1521, systematised and elucidated Luther's
theology as he had expounded it in his lectures on the *Epistle to the
Romans*. The book, translated into German by Spalatin, went through
17 editions within four years of its publication. The religious orders
provided him with many supporters; from his own order, the Augustinian Friars, Link, Lang, Zwilling, Guttel, Jacob Probst and Heinrich
Moller. Eberlin and Myconius had been Franciscans; Bucer was a
former Dominican. Not all the clerical recruits were a credit to the
movement, for the new-found freedom of the Gospel became an
invitation to the antinomianism which Luther so condemned. But
the general level, though it included hot-heads and radicals, was
surprisingly high. If Lutheranism now and again attracted the dregs
of the proletariat in its wake, the majority of its leaders were devoted,
conscientious men, intent on proclaiming what they sincerely believed
to be the Word of God from their pulpits. It was perhaps plain that
they were not always agreed as to the interpretation of the Word; but
the movement of protest against the old religion gathered momentum
in the 1520s. Within a few years Lutheran teaching had spread to
Strasbourg and Ulm, to Constance and Augsburg, to Breslau and
Nordlingen, to Hamburg and Bremen. In north-west Germany the
Bishop of Samland accepted Luther's views.

The secular powers were slow to reveal their hands. The princes,
undoubtedly suspicious of innovations which threatened the existing
structure of society, were waiting to see whether Lutheranism could
be utilised to their political advantage. The Elector of Saxony, balanced
uneasily on the fence, had taken a more definite lead to support Luther
than most of his colleagues in the college of princes; but his brother,
John, and his nephew, John Frederick, were more open in their
acceptance of evangelical teaching. His cousin, Duke George of Saxony,
on the other hand, was an outright opponent. An increasing number

of the greater and lesser nobility had been won over to Luther's teaching, some impressed by his principles and others attracted by the possibility of taking over Church property, with the object of bolstering their own failing economy, their static revenues at a time of steadily rising prices.

The Edict of Worms for all its solemn phraseology had remained a dead letter. The Imperial Diet had reassembled at Nuremberg in November, 1522, and was technically in session until March, 1523. The affable and sybaritic Leo X had died in 1521. His successor was a very different man, Charles V's old tutor, Adrian Dedel. Pope Adrian VI was by inclination a conservative scholar but he was also a sincere, well-meaning man who was anxious to eliminate corruption from the Church. On the other hand, as a former Inquisitor-General, he detested heresy. While, therefore, he was ready to recognise the abuses which tarnished the body of Christ, he was as inflexible as his predecessors where Luther was concerned. Yet his very willingness to undertake reform and even to sponsor a summons to a General Council greatly eased the task of his delegate to the Diet of Nuremberg, the Bishop of Tirano, Chierigati. The considerable expansion of Lutheranism made the Estates chary of enforcing the edict. In February, 1523, the Diet decided by a majority vote that it was indeed inexpedient to attempt to do so. Once more they enumerated the abuses from which the Church was suffering and urged the calling of a General Council in Germany in which the laity would be represented. If this request was granted, they agreed to ask the Elector of Saxony to prevent Luther and his followers from publishing controversial pamphlets and books and to ensure that married clergy and apostate religious would be punished by ecclesiastical courts. This was perhaps a small return for the profession of faith to the Pope and the Emperor with which the document started.

In any case the proceedings of the Diet of Nuremberg were doomed to disappointment. The unhappy but excellent Pope soon died and was succeeded by an amiable and incompetent diplomat, the Medici, Clement VII, whose native disinclination to reform was strengthened by his dislike of the Hapsburgs. Cardinal Campeggio who represented him at the Diet when it reassembled at Nuremberg in early 1524 again demanded the execution of the Edict of Worms. The majority, alarmed perhaps at the growing extent of Lutheran influence, agreed that the edict ought to be imposed 'as far as it was possible' to do so, but they reiterated their request for the calling of a General Council. Indeed, to bring pressure to bear on the Pope, they actually arranged

that a German council should meet at Speyer in the coming autumn to examine Luther's teaching and to draw up a list of the errors it doubtless contained. Campeggio protested strongly at such a notion and the Emperor himself effectively brought the proceedings to an end by forbidding the proposed German council to meet and ordering the enforcement of the Edict of Worms. The history of the Diet would indeed seem fruitless as well as tedious if it were not possible to discern the steady growth within it of Lutheran and anti-Lutheran groups. In the summer of 1524 a number of Catholic princes and churchmen met together at Ratisbon to discuss how the Church could be protected and preserved against its dangerous critic.

Luther was more than ever in the European limelight and in spite of occasional depressions and tensions no less confident of his divinely-supported position. 'The doctrine of Luther', the Emperor's young brother, Ferdinand, told him on January 27th, 1523, 'has taken such deep root throughout the whole empire, that to-day among every 1,000 persons there is not one who is not to some extent touched by it'. Luther himself felt that he could now afford to ignore the Emperor whom he had once revered as the Lord's anointed, dismissing him as a 'maggot-sack'. With Melanchthon, he concocted a peculiarly vulgar little satire entitled the *Interpretation of the Pope-Ass found at Rome and the Monks Calf at Freiburg*. Such scurrilous literature afforded a similar satisfaction to the reader as does modern pornography, with which it had some association. Yet it would be unfair to judge either reformer by *esprits* of this sort. Within three years of the Diet of Worms, Luther had initiated a mighty religious revolution. Whether he could, however, impose the presumed standards of the apostolic age on the Church of sixteenth-century Germany was still evidently a very open question.

CHAPTER 7

Consolidation and Controversy
1524–1529

The pattern of Luther's daily existence was now settled. While he was the centre, indeed the storm-centre, of a series of different conflicts, disputes between Roman and Lutheran, quarrels between humanists and Lutherans, his private life had a static quality. He was never a peripatetic preacher like Wesley. Indeed his experience of travel was comparatively limited. Apart from his early visit to Rome, the memory of which became more vivid with the passing of the years, he never moved outside Germany, and to an increasing extent rarely outside Saxony. This stability may help to explain some of the limitations of his personality and even of his influence. He lacked the cosmopolitan quality which, for instance, John Calvin possessed. Throughout his life he remained a typical German, the grandson of Saxon peasants, at the close of his life physically thick-set, for a middle-aged spread gave the former lean, ascetic monk the appearance of a buxom *hausfrau*, a hearty eater and drinker, not averse to bawdy witticisms, and outwardly lacking the qualities of sanctity and devotion. The burly frame, however, housed a man of deep spiritual feeling as well as a character which was never fully free from neurotic tensions. Although his intellect was of exceptional power, he was not a man of wide culture. He loved music intensely, and continued to play the lute as he had done as a student, but the glories of Renaissance literature and art passed him by. He readily used the tools of contemporary humanism but to illuminate the Bible for the common reader. Beneath the university professor, Martin remained the German peasant-farmer, rooted in the soil—he enjoyed gardening and had for his time an unusual appreciation of natural beauty—and limited in his personality and outlook by stock, environment and upbringing.

Luther's domestic character, if it can be so termed, had been enhanced by his marriage. Although Luther professed to have had no interest in women while he had been in the monastery, his disturbed state may have been stimulated by sexual difficulties, very probably by masturbation. In his *Address to the German Nobility* he had in part rested his argument in favour of clerical marriage on the difficulty that so many priests had in living a life of sexual abstinence. A kind of eliminative sexuality appears in the references to the waste products of the body and anal action scattered about his works, as also possibly in his obsessive hatred of celibacy. This had not been at first apparent. The monastic life had made too strong an impression to enable him to approve Carlstadt's encouragement of monks and nuns to marry; but he rapidly came to terms with the situation. In 1523 he helped to abduct 12 nuns who wished to leave the cloister; 'a wagon load of vestal virgins has just come to town, all more eager for marriage than for life. God grant them husbands lest worse befall.' Spalatin hinted that Luther himself might find a possible bride among them, and the reformer replied cheerfully enough that: 'As to what you write about my marrying, do not be surprised that I do not wed, even if I am so famous a lover. You should be more surprised when I write so much about marriage and in this way have so much to do with women that I do not turn into a woman, let alone marry one.' Within less than two years all the nine nuns who lived in Wittenberg found husbands except one, Katharine von Bora. As she was working as a domestic servant, she would gladly have taken a husband and Luther readily did what he could to help her, but without success. He suggested a Dr.

Glatz whom Katharine found repulsive. She told Amsdorf that she would much prefer to marry him or even Luther himself. Luther was not averse to the idea of married life but he could not pretend that he was in love with Katharine. 'I am ready. I believe in marriage, and I intend to get married before I die, even though it should be only a betrothal like Joseph's.'

The marriage took place in the presence of his aged parents on June 27th, 1525. Luther had in part married to please his father (whose attempt to make him abandon the celibate life of a monk he had frustrated as a young man) who wanted grandchildren, and in part to spite the Pope and the Devil. Luther was now 42 and his bride was 26. Notwithstanding all the omens the marriage was a great success. Luther had lived the life of the abstracted don, insufficiently exacting to care very much about his creature comforts or the necessary trivialities of ordinary daily existence. His wife created a home; 'before I was married the bed was not made for a whole year and became foul with sweat. But I worked so hard and was so weary I tumbled in without it.' There can be little doubt that he enjoyed the physical experience of marriage, countering his earlier sexual tensions, and delighted in the birth of a numerous progeny: Hans in 1526, Elizabeth in 1527, Magdalena in 1529, Martin in 1531, Paul in 1533 and Margaretha in 1534. 'There is about to be born the child of a monk and a nun', he wrote shortly before Hans' birth, 'Such a child must have a great Lord for a godfather.' There were certainly occasions when he found the presence of young children an irritant, but the worries of family life were compensated by its joys.

Luther's views of marriage were conventional. He believed that the husband was the natural superior to whom the wife owed love and obedience. 'Women', he declared, 'were created with large hips so that they should stay at home and sit on them.' Children must obey their parents, a principle that Luther continuously stressed, remembering his disobedience to his father. Yet he very well understood that marriage had to be a partnership. Inevitably there were occasional rifts but there can be little doubt that the more he lived with Katie the more he loved her.

In some respects if marriage eased his way of life, it created economic problems. At first neither he nor his wife appear to have had a sufficient income to support his growing family and other members of his household. To supplement their finances, the Luthers took in student boarders, whose experience of their landlord's conversation later formed the material for the fascinating but not wholly reliable

27 Martin Luther
From a portrait by
Lucas Cranach the Elder, c. 1526

28 Katharine von Bora
From a portrait by
s Cranach the Elder, c. 1526

29   The Reformers
Detail of the Epitaph of Meienburg by
Lucas Cranach the Elder

The figures depicted, from left to right in the foreground, are Luther,
Bugenhagen, Erasmus, Justus Jonas, Cruciger and Spalatin

Table Talk. Yet Luther had a more than adequate professional stipend. The monastery which the Elector gave him on his marriage was sold by his children in 1564 for 3,700 gulden. He bought the Zulsdorf farm from Katie's brother in 1540 for 610 gulden. Like other members of the academic faculty he was in general exempt from taxation. He was in receipt of gifts in kind and money from the Elector and other princes. The Elector contributed 600 gulden towards the purchase of the Zulsdorf farm and gave materials towards improving the farm buildings. Albert, Duke of Prussia, gave him a wedding present of 20 gulden. Henry VIII sent him 50 gulden in 1535, an ironical gift from a king who had once earned the Pope's favour for refuting his opinions. Although he did not get the profits from his books, he had grants of free wood and grain and the fees from presiding over university disputations. A tax assessment of 1542 indicates that he owned real estate worth 9,000 gulden but owed debts of some 450. He certainly died a comparatively wealthy man. If he was occasionally short of money, it must have been in part the result of his generous hospitality. Luther himself worked in the cloister garden and his hard-working wife looked after an orchard, a fishpond and a small farm. Yet, all in all, he had no regrets. 'My Katie', he told a friend after a year's experience of married life, 'is in all things so obliging and pleasing to me that I could not exchange my poverty for the riches of Croesus.' She cared for the household, saw to his wants, brought up his children, worked on his farm and nursed him in his not infrequent bouts of ill-health. She was there to console him when he was overwhelmed by depression and despair. Indeed he wondered from time to time whether his affection for his wife and family was not inordinate: 'I give more credit to Katharine than to Christ, who has done so much more for me.'

It was as well that Luther should have his domestic oasis, since there was no diminution in the number of the problems which confronted him. The Catholics, controlled, as he believed them to be, by dark, satanic forces, were a constant and known enemy. He still talked in terms of imminent death or martyrdom, but it seemed an unlikely prospect. If the Catholic princes showed some signs of coming together in an offensive alliance in defence of their faith, the Emperor was not in a sufficiently strong position to impose the Edict of Worms. The Elector of Saxony was ailing, but his brother and nephew were good friends to Luther and much more actively sympathetic to Protestant teaching; John Frederick was more likely to take up the sword in defence of the Lutherans than his uncle.

In fact the more immediate problems were created by the spread of Lutheranism. Its comparatively inchoate doctrine, its as yet undeveloped organisation and the somewhat intolerant enthusiasm of its leaders provided ample opportunity for friction. Their only recognised authority was the Word of God which, as theologians have long known, can be indeterminate and oracular and is no easy guide to action. As long as Luther was himself its principal exponent, interpretation was no difficult matter; but the sense of Scripture can only be properly determined by a man 'who has experience of the subject-matter' itself. His approach was not subjective, but it was in part conditioned by his spiritual development. There were, however, other scholars at work who developed notions that differed from his own, so straining charity and tolerance. His former colleague, Andreas Carlstadt, whose innovations at Wittenberg had led to Luther's return there, was initiating far-reaching changes at Orlamünde where he was now parish priest. He criticised the belief in the real presence of Christ in the Eucharist, insisting that since God is spirit it is ludicrous to assert that He can in any fashion be said to be present through the bread and wine. He rejected infant baptism on the grounds that it has no effective meaning until the Christian has experienced new birth. He proclaimed the priesthood of all believers, maintaining that ministers ought not to be distinguished from the laity either by insignia or clothes and should earn their living by trade or other occupations. Such left-wing Puritanism, for Carlstadt was a strong opponent of organs and images as well as a fervent sabbatarian, was much to Luther's distaste. He sought to counter Carlstadt's teaching with scriptural citations but it was soon very apparent that this was a game that two, and more than two could play at, with increasing acerbity.

There was, however, a much more disagreeable and dangerous preacher in the reformed camp in the person of Thomas Münzer. Münzer, a Thuringian born in 1488 or 1489, was a learned man, a university graduate versed in Greek and Hebrew but evidently 'a man born for schism and heresies', eagerly absorbing patristic writings (from Hegisippus he borrowed the notion that the Church was the community of believers) and other prophetic works such as the Pseudo-Joachite commentary on Jeremiah which seems to have made him wonder whether he too might not be a prophet of God. After various religious doubts he had embraced Luther's teaching, but the breach with orthodoxy soon brought him into strange waters. At Zwickau he made contact with the weaver, Nicholas Storch, who had adopted the chiliastic ideas of the old Taborite group in Bohemia. He came to believe that the true Christian, a member of the elect, was directly illuminated by God. He did not even require the Word of God in the Scriptures since he was in direct communion with God and inspired by Him. 'The letter killeth but the Spirit giveth life.' The Scriptures were to be regarded simply as the manuscript, 'Bible, Babel, Bubble' which lacked authority without an inspired expounder, but the expounder was inspired not by the Scriptures but directly by God. He distinguished between the historical Christ and the living, inner or spiritual Christ, the true redeemer, who came to dwell in the soul of the elect. Yet the *via dolorosa* of the historical Christ culminating in the saving experience of the Cross afforded the pattern of life for his followers; the Christian life, Münzer firmly held, inevitably entailed suffering. But the suffering was placed against the divine inspiration which upheld the elect and which made their final victory inevitable. The reborn in the spirit will recognise each other and so create a covenant of the elect, who will in turn institute the kingdom of God. Münzer and his followers were confident that they were living in the last days. They were perhaps a little unsure as to the course of events. Some foresaw the conquest of the world by the Turks and the victory of Antichrist; but none of them doubted that the righteous would ultimately exterminate the godless. They took to heart the more bloody types of the Old Testament story, the slaying of the prophets of Baal by Elijah, the slaughter of the sons of Ahab by Jehu and the murder of Sisera by Jael, and incorporated them in the fantastic imagery of the Book of Revelation.

Their assured, prophetic teaching had made a great impression on Zwickau, a small industrial town in the centre of silver mines which had attracted a landless proletariat, smitten by the adverse economic conditions created by over-production and rising prices. Münzer led the attack on the local preacher, a follower of Luther, who had the favour of the prosperous burghers. The town council, faced by the threat of disorder, intervened and expelled the prophets, three of whom then made their way to Wittenberg while Münzer himself went to nearby Bohemia. Münzer's innovations had been drastic and revolutionary; infant baptism, the sacraments, the priesthood were eliminated to make way for the guidance of the Holy Spirit. The kingdom of God would be seized by violence. Everything that he learned about his teaching outraged Luther, its rejection of a divinely-appointed magistracy through whom the Church could be reformed, its opposition to church order, its theological radicalism; while for Münzer Luther became more and more 'Dr. Easychair and Dr.

Pussyfoot', 'Brother Soft Life', 'Dr. Liar', the man whose doctrine of justification by faith was no more worthy of respect than the papists' doctrine of justification by works.

But what could Luther do to stem the spread of this aberrant teaching? Münzer made his way to Prague where he declared that he was the prophet of the living Word, the *nuntius Christi* inspired by God, but if he had expected the land of John Hus to view his preposterous claims in kindly fashion he was disappointed. The town council expelled the prophet, who after enduring great hardship came to the small Thuringian town of Allstedt near Eisleben where he was appointed parish priest at St. John's Church. 'The living God is sharpening his scythe in me, so that later I can cut down the red poppies and the blue cornflowers.' At Allstedt he reformed the church and introduced the first liturgy in the German language, *Das Deutsche Kirchenamt* (1523) and *Deutsche Evangelische Messe* (1524), in some respects restrained and sensible; the words of consecration were repeated by the whole congregation as a 'royal-priestly' people. He married a former nun and made a name for himself as a preacher, organising his followers into a 'League of the Elect' which had revolutionary possibilities; in March, 1524, they attacked and destroyed the image of the Virgin in the Mellerbach Chapel, which belonged to the convent of Naundorf, to which the townsfolk of Allstedt had to pay feudal dues. He wrote to Luther, stressing the significance of the indwelling spirit in the work of redemption but acknowledging the importance of revelation through the Scriptures. 'When the spirit of truth is come he shall guide you into all truth', he quoted from St. John; but Luther told Spalatin that his irritating correspondent was either 'mad or drunk'.

Münzer was certainly intoxicated with his own visionary enthusiasm. His teaching that revelation is not something to be found simply in the Bible but forms an experience which the elect soul can himself enjoy made a great impression on the weavers, miners and peasants of the locality. The immanent Word of God could be as well manifested through an unlettered peasant as a doctor of theology. Moreover the Elect had the key to the door of salvation; they are the saints to whom God will consign the kingdom after the imminent destruction of the ungodly. In July, 1524, he preached a sermon before the Elector's brother, Duke John, and his son John Frederick, in which he announced the coming end of the world and called on the Saxon princes to assist in the work of destroying the ungodly. 'Drive Christ's enemies out from amongst the Elect, for you are the instruments for that purpose.

. . . The sword is necessary to exterminate them. . . . At the harvest-time one must pluck the weeds out of God's vineyard. . . . But the angels who are sharpening their sickles for that work are no other than the earnest servants of God. . . . For the ungodly have no right to live farther than the elect shall accord them.' But the princes needed an adviser, a prophet, as Nebuchadnezzar required the services of Daniel. Clearly Münzer was concerned that he should replace Luther in the Saxon princes' confidence, perhaps aware that Duke John, at least, under the influence of his court preacher, Wolfgang Stein, tended to favour extreme opinions.

Luther was anxious, as well he might be. He wrote to the Elector and his brother, urging them to take action against the false prophet. 'You must banish the offender from the land. Our office is simply preaching and suffering. Christ and the apostles did not smash images and churches, but won hearts with God's word. The Old Testament slaughter of the ungodly is not to be imitated. If these Allstedters want to wipe out the ungodly, they will have to bathe in blood.' This would indeed have seemed precisely the liquid in which Münzer would have been most at home. The Saxon princes were extraordinarily dilatory in dealing with the spreading infection; but the Elector's nephew, John Frederick, admitted that he was 'having a terrible time with the Satan of Allstedt. . . . The sword which is ordained of God to punish the evil must be used with energy. Carlstadt also is stirring up something, and the Devil wants to be Lord.' Carlstadt, increasingly sympathetic to Münzer's views, was turned out of Saxony, declaring that Luther was now in his opinion a cousin of Antichrist. As a result of Luther's representations Münzer was summoned to Weimar to explain his conduct.

The events of the next few months revealed his lack of mental balance. In his pamphlet *The explicit unmasking of the false belief of the faithless world,* Münzer showed that he had not given up any hope of the princes' help in the work of regeneration. 'The powerful, self-willed unbelievers must be put down from their seats because they hinder the holy, genuine Christian faith in themselves and in the whole world, when it is trying to emerge in all its true, original force.' He was beginning to believe that if the millennium was to be inaugurated, the poor were the potential Elect who could be used to that end under his own divinely-inspired leadership. 'In truth, many of them will have to be roused, so that with the greatest possible zeal and with passionate earnestness they may sweep Christendom clean of ungodly rulers.' He did not propose any immediate social amelioration but he almost certainly felt that when the new Church, the kingdom of God, was established, it would be an egalitarian, communist society. *The most amply called-for defence and answer to the unspiritual soft-living flesh at Wittenberg* was aimed at Luther whom he now identified as the beast of the Apocalypse. In it he vigorously attacked dominion and property, which by right should be alone at the disposal of the Elect, which Luther purposely defended. 'The wretched flatterer is silent . . . about the origin of all theft. . . . Look, the seed-grounds of usury and theft and robbery are our lords and princes, they take all creatures as their property: the fish in the water, the birds·in the air, the plants on the ground have all got to be theirs.' The princes exercised great patience, but even Münzer must have realised that his reception was not wholly favourable and escaping by night over the walls of Allstedt he made his way to Mühlhausen, a free Imperial city, where taking advantage of a high degree of unemployment and poverty he joined the ex-monk, Pfeiffer, in a radical revolution. Luther wrote to the municipal authorities who for other good reasons expelled the turbulent preachers in September, 1524. After wandering through south Germany, inveighing against Luther and preaching the doctrine of immediate inspiration and the need for slaughtering the ungodly, he arrived back at Mühlhausen, where Pfeiffer had meanwhile engineered the election of a new town council favourable to his teaching.

His return coincided with the mutterings which were soon to burst into bloody revolt. The Peasants' War was one of those tragic, spontaneous, social eruptions which occur from time to time in the history of propertied and hierarchically ordered societies. As with the revolt of the peasants in England in 1381 no one reason satisfactorily explains the series of regional disturbances which came to a head in 1525. The occasion for one such rising was the demand made by the Countess of Lupfen on her estates at Stühlingen in June, 1524, south-west of the Black Forest, to collect strawberries and snail shells (on which to wind her silks) when the peasants wanted to gather in the harvest. In some sense agrarian unrest had been an endemic feature of rural society since the steady disintegration of the feudal order, a movement powerfully affected in Germany as elsewhere by the plagues of the fourteenth century, subsequent depopulation, the break-up of great estates and increasing emancipation. By and large the condition of the peasant improved· steadily. He was personally free, bound only to render certain tenurial payments, and he was in enjoyment of a steadily rising wage which in a time of static prices enabled him to experience considerable material prosperity. The economic developments of the early sixteenth century had not proved necessarily disadvantageous. The rise in the population, together with external factors such as the greater availability of silver, from the south German mines and later from Spanish America, brought about a steep increase in the prices of agrarian produce, which stimulated farming. One of the first objects of the peasants in the subsequent troubles seems to have been to secure a greater degree of self-government; they bargained with the spiritual and temporal lords to win greater autonomy.

On the other side of the coin two developments fostered trouble. The greater princes took every possible advantage to create a strong, centralised administration in their estates, overriding local custom, increasing taxation and substituting Roman law for traditional law. The creation of new, orderly, absolutist principalities threatened the peasants' traditional liberties. Many noble landowners were still suffering from the agrarian recession of the later Middle Ages. Peasant tenure was protected in law from increases in rents. The German lords were thus often unable to raise their rents to compensate for the fall in the value of money as a result of the slow price rise; all they could do was to try to improve the profits of direct farming by better methods of cultivation, and in general by seeking a more effective exploitation of their rights. In particular they took advantage of Roman law to override peasant rights in respect of some of the facilities such as the use of communal woods, streams and meadows, which immemorial custom provided for the peasants.

The peasant disturbances of 1524–5 were not the reaction of an oppressed social class driven to revolution by new exactions, as much as the response of a people who had and enjoyed an increasing degree of freedom and prosperity threatened by what has been termed the 'legally just and materially insignificant demands by the lords which the latter, in trying to arrest their decline, were exacting more completely and intensively than in the preceding era.' Economic and social factors do not, however, alone explain the outbreak of violence. Astrologers had predicted that 1524, when all the planets were in the constellation of the fish, would be a year of great disturbances; more than 50 tracts on this subject alone had been published in 1523. Legend and rumour, a peculiarly effective agent in periods of social disturbance, fostered stories of apocalyptic hopes, of the victory of social justice over oppression and wrong. There was a strong element of proletarian religion in the peasants' demands; the labourer's symbols, the hammer, the sickle and the *bundschuh*, surrounded the crucifix. Luther's teaching, with its condemnation of the Pope and curia, its

149

attack on the monasteries and its assertion of the priesthood of all believers, must have filtered through to many of the peasants. Münzer's apocalyptic preaching made an obvious appeal.

The Catholics then and later declared that Luther was partly responsible for the trouble. A *bundschuh* had been appended to one of the placards supporting Luther when he had been at Worms in 1521. A contemporary woodcut depicted him sitting garbed in armour before a fire, greasing the *bundschuh* preparatory to putting it on. The Twelve Articles, perhaps the most articulate expression of the peasants' demands, contained clauses that seemed to echo his ideas, the right of the congregation to choose or eject the minister who is there to 'preach the Holy Gospel without human addition', the utilisation of tithes, except for a modest amount set aside to support the minister, to relieve the poor, the abolition of the little tithe on cattle; but their basic claims, the right to the use of the common fields, woods and streams, the right to hunt and to fish, to take free wood for fuel and building, the abolition of feudal burdens like mortuary and heriot, represented rights which they had already won from their landlords and which they believed to be threatened anew.

The disturbances were wide-ranging and unco-ordinated. The peasants plundered castles and monasteries—70 monasteries were destroyed in Thuringia and 52 in Franconia—killed bailiffs and raped nuns, caught game and emptied fish ponds. In the first days of the troubles peasant communities used the threat of violence to extract privileges from their local lords; but as time went on the peasants seemed to lose a sense of purpose. They seldom knew what they wanted. They were fascinated by violence, drunk on free wine and beer, gorged with looted food, stimulated by firing castles and ravishing nuns. The established order, equally unprepared and unorganized, caught by surprise, had to draw breath before the rebound. Sometimes the peasants were led by men of their own class, but knights were occasionally involved.

The Thuringian peasants found a leader in Thomas Münzer (though his active association with the revolt was brief), who had made good use of his recently formed League of the Elect, whom he exhorted with glowing speeches, promising an egalitarian paradise as soon as the ungodly had been liquidated. 'Luther', he told his gaping audience, 'says that the poor people have enough in their faith. Doesn't he see that usury and taxes impede the reception of the faith? He claims that the Word of God is sufficient. Doesn't he realise that men whose every moment is consumed in the making of a living have no time to learn to read the Word of God? The princes bleed the people with usury and count as their own the fish in the stream, the bird in the air, and the grass of the field, and Dr. Liar says "Amen!" What courage has he, Dr. Pussyfoot, the new pope of Wittenberg, Dr. Easychair, the basking sycophant! He says there should be no rebellion because the sword has been committed by God to the ruler, but the power of the sword belongs to the whole community. In the good old days the people stood by when judgment was rendered lest the ruler pervert justice. They shall be cast down from their seats. The fowls of the heavens are gathering to devour their carcasses.'

The princes gradually regained their poise. The Elector of Saxony had died on May 4th, but his successor, his brother, John, joined with other princes to appeal to the youthful Philip of Hesse, who had already a considerable reputation as a soldier. He marched towards Thuringia as the chief centre of disaffection. The peasants were encamped at Frankenhausen whence they appealed to Münzer to lead them. Münzer, preening himself as a new Gideon, made up in assurance what he lacked in military skill. When the Prince demanded that the peasants should surrender their erstwhile leader, he managed to persuade them that the lord of hosts had promised victory. 'He would', he shouted passionately, 'catch the enemy's cannon balls in his own cloak.' A rainbow, the symbol on his banner, suddenly appeared in the sky to confirm his promises; but the lord of hosts was lamentably absent when the princes ordered the cannons to fire. The peasants fled in panic, and a defeat became a massacre. Münzer was discovered in hiding, tortured and beheaded a few days later. Elsewhere the established order, its confidence returning, its soldiers well armed, defeated the crude peasant bands, executed the ringleaders and reasserted the control of the landlords.

Luther's attitude to the peasants has to be understood within the context of the contemporary situation. He was himself of peasant stock and he undoubtedly believed that some of their demands were justified; but his very identification with the peasant class made him eager to disown their revolutionary movement. He was an academic who held fast to the medieval veneration for order and harmony as attributes of God himself. He believed that the magistrate was God's representative upon whom rested the responsibility for sponsoring the Reformation itself. In rebelling against his authority and in fermenting social disorder the peasants were striking at the roots of a divinely ordered society. He was eager to repudiate his own alleged association with the rebellion, and undoubtedly desirous of bringing retribution

151

Wider die Mordischen
vnd Reubischen Rotten der Bawren.

hab got lieb

Psalm. vij.
Seyne tück werden jñ selbs treffen/
Vnd seyn mütwill/ wirdt vber jñ außgeen?

1525.
Martinus Luther. Wittemberg.

30 The title-page of Luther's tract, *Against the Thievish and Murderous Hordes of Peasants*, 1525

From Bainton, 'Here I Stand', Abingdon Press

to the impertinent and obnoxious Münzer. He was worried that the Evangelical reform movement might itself fall a victim to current disorder unless the princes took rapid and violent action to suppress the rebels. In such an emergency force was the only conceivable answer. To encourage the princes he wrote his savage tract, *Against the Thievish and Murderous Hordes of Peasants*. He declared that the rebellion was diabolic in origin; the authorities were in truth warring 'not with flesh and blood but with spiritual wickedness', not on this occasion in such high places. Weakness and conciliation would only encourage the rebels. 'If the peasant is in open rebellion, then he is outside the law of God, for rebellion is not simply murder, but it is like a great fire which attacks and lays waste a whole land. Thus, rebellion brings with it a land full of murders and bloodshed, makes widows and orphans, and turns everything upside down like a great disaster. Therefore, let everyone who can, smite, slay and stab, secretly or openly, remembering that nothing can be more poisonous, hurtful, or devilish than a rebel. It is just as when one must kill a mad dog; if you don't strike him, he will strike you, and the whole land with you.' Later he wrote another pamphlet, *An Open Letter concerning the Hard Book against the Peasants*, in which he justified the use of force but added: 'I had two fears: if the peasants became lords, the devil would become abbot; but if these tyrannical princes become lords, the devil's mother would become abbess.' He urged then that the peasants should be treated mercifully and called on the landlords to defer their vengeance.

Nothing can justify the shrill and savage tone of Luther's original tract, but it must be remembered that he believed the Evangelical Reformation was itself imperilled by the ravaging bands. The pamphlet was written as the flames burned castles and manor houses not so very distant from Wittenberg itself. The impact of the Peasants' War on the future of Lutheranism was important. The Catholics continued to hold Luther in part responsible for the outbreak of the revolt. The peasants certainly felt that Luther had betrayed their cause and so far as they were attracted to Protestant teaching were drawn to join the ranks of the more socially-advanced Anabaptists rather than the conservative Lutherans. Luther himself had been deeply shocked by the outburst. He had not himself realised the possible implications of his own teaching about the priesthood of believers and the ultimate authority of the congregation. He was led to stress more than he had done in the past the authority of the just ruler and the citizen's obligation to obey him.

Luther experienced criticism from a different quarter during the year of the peasants' revolt. His relations with the humanists had never been particularly close, though both sought a return to the conditions of primitive Christianity, in part by using the linguistic techniques which enabled a more literal interpretation of the Scriptures. But while Luther greatly appreciated their outright denunciation of scholasticism, religion was his forte rather than humanism. He was not indeed an opponent of learning any more than he was hostile to human reason if it was kept within its proper limits. Learning, and this included classical literature as well as straightforward theological studies, was a part of the necessary stock-in-trade of the good Christian minister. 'Do not give way to your apprehension', he wrote in March, 1523, to Eobanus Hessus who had expressed his alarm at the apparent contempt for learning shown by the reformers, 'lest we Germans become more barbarous than ever we were by reason of the decline of letters through our theology. I am persuaded that, without a skilled training in literary studies, no true theology can establish and maintain itself.' A year later he told Strauss that 'I am convinced that the neglect of education will bring the greatest ruin to the Gospel'.

In similar fashion, as we have already noted, Luther was prepared to use the human reason. Certainly he sometimes gave the impression that he condemned heartily those who used dialectic; reason was 'carnal', 'stupid', 'the Devil's whore'. Natural reason, however, acting within the framework of the earthly kingdom, is a gift from God and regenerate reason, subject to the Word of God, is the handmaid of faith. Reason is an excellent quality if it is used by regenerate man. By itself it is powerless to lead a man to salvation.

Such qualifications help to explain his attitude to humanist scholarship. While he esteemed learning and believed that it was a necessary tool, its ultimate efficacy depended on the extent to which it served as the instrument of faith, captive to Christ. This attitude made it fundamentally difficult to reach an accommodation with the humanists, whose leading representative was the cosmopolitan Dutch scholar, Erasmus. He was 17 years older than Luther, an acknowledged master in the field of contemporary learning who had done more than anyone else to discredit the hold of the scholastic method and to restore the text of the Greek Testament and the patristic writings to the attention of the literate public. He was besides a trenchant critic of existing abuses in the Church. His *Praise of Folly* was an acute satire on the monastic life (from which he was almost as much as Luther an apostate); he poured scorn on the worship of relics and even (through the unacknowledged *Julius Exclusus*) on the Pope himself. But in spite of his atrabilious nature his writings show that he did not lack spiritual depth and genuine Christian devotion. No man, it could be claimed, did more to prepare the way for Luther or was more fitted at first sight to co-operate with him. Yet he correctly adjudged the situation when he commented: 'I laid a hen's egg: Luther hatched a bird of quite different breed.'

There was a basic divergence between Luther and the humanists. Erasmus wanted a reform of the Church, the removal of its abuses and a return to the primitive faith of the early Christians. He wished to recover the Christ of the Gospels without a dogmatic revolution. He did not criticise the doctrine of the Church, its sacraments, its priesthood or its hierarchy. Least of all did he believe in the use of violence and force. 'I am averse', he said, 'to any action which might lead to commotion and uproar.' Temperamentally a man of peace (though not in words) he deplored war and aggression or indeed any radical disturbance of the social and religious order. Nor could he accept the seemingly exaggerated emphasis which Luther placed on justification by faith. Fundamentally, in spite of much that they had in common, the two men were in character and purpose antithetically opposed. Erasmus was the true scholar, the great Latin stylist, the friend of the great world, averse to enthusiasm and extremism, cool, almost sceptical in his attitude, tending to conceal the under-current of genuine spirituality which gave life to his personality. Whereas Luther, with a longer, richer and ultimately more fruitful experience of monastic life than Erasmus, was almost exclusively concerned with religion, Erasmus' interests were very much wider. Erasmus was never a true monk, but Luther in a certain fashion never escaped the impress of his monastic training. He remained a monk or at least a monk *manqué* who in spite of his domestic life had a single objective, not in its ultimate purpose so different from that of the dedicated religious.

At first there was a somewhat uneasy alliance between the two men. Although Luther was aware that Erasmus paid more attention to the works of Jerome and Origen than to those of Augustine, he referred to the scholar as 'our Erasmus', and the latter expressed his approval of the 95 theses and his attack on indulgences. He specifically commended him to the protection of the Elector of Saxony. Later Erasmus wrote an outspoken letter to the Archbishop of Mainz denouncing the Church's policy of persecution: 'Men who above all others it beseems to practise meekness seem to thirst for nothing else but human blood, so eager are they that Luther should be seized and destroyed. Their conduct is worthy of the butcher, not the theologian.' He held that it was unjustifiable to denounce as heretical those who simply take issue on 'certain questions on which the schoolmen have always disputed and even doubted'. 'Nowadays, if anyone differs from Thomas Aquinas, he is decried as a heretic; nay, he is a heretic if he demurs to any disputatious effusion which some sophist yesterday fabricated in the schools. Whatever they don't like, whatever they don't understand is heresy. To know Greek is heresy. Whatever they do not do themselves is heresy.'

Erasmus, however, soon realised that there was a divergence between his attitude and that of Luther. While both he and Luther rejected the scholastic method, Luther had adopted a dogmatic Augustinianism which Erasmus found repugnant. He was horrified by the threat of violence implied in Luther's teaching. 'I certainly would rather have Luther corrected than destroyed', he wrote in March, 1521, 'but I shall not oppose if they roast or boil him. The fall of one man is a small matter, but I am very much concerned for the public tranquillity.' Moreover while he sympathised with Luther's denunciation of corrupt practices, he came to the reluctant conclusion that his teaching was in fact hardly in accord with Christian orthodoxy. He was worried too that rumour identified his own ideas with those of Luther. He may well have feared, for Erasmus was a self-regarding man, that he might lose his patrons' good will. He was angered by Hutten's attack on his conservatism and the charge of cowardice.

Luther was hardly better pleased. 'The human', he had written as early as March, 1517, 'avails more with Erasmus than the divine.' He did indeed think that Erasmus was a coward. He believed that he was insufficiently serious and too facetious in his treatment of matters that Luther regarded as unsuitable for witty comment. He esteemed his scholarship but thought that he had entirely neglected the religious significance of the text; 'He has damaged the Gospel just as much as he has advanced grammar.' He suspected that his plea of friendship was not genuine. 'Better', he declared, 'an open enemy than a false friend.' '*Melior est Eccius*', he wrote to Spalatin in May, 1522, '*eo qui aperta fronte hostem profitetur. Hunc autem tergiversantem et subdolum, tum amicum, tum hostem detestor.*' 'What Erasmus holds or feigns to believe in spiritual things', he told Oecolampadius a year later, 'both his early and his recent books abundantly testify. . . . He has performed the work for which he was destined. He has furthered the study of the classics and recalled men from impious sophistry. Perhaps like Moses he will die in the land of Moab, for to the higher pursuit of spiritual things he cannot lead.' Unfortunately a copy of this letter came into Erasmus' hands, and he was naturally very angry.

The real breach in their relations had thus occurred long before 1524, but the publication of Erasmus' *De Libero Arbitrio*, printed by Froben of Basle during the summer, made the break final. 'The die is cast', Erasmus wrote to Henry VIII (to whom he had sent a presentation copy, as also to Pope Clement VII, Wolsey and others of his noble patrons), 'my book on free will has seen the light. An audacious villany, as things now stand in Germany!' In this Erasmus challenged Luther's doctrine of justification by faith with learning and irony, and without undue vituperation. Luther replied in *De Servo Arbitrio*, a vigorous vindication of his beliefs. Where Erasmus used a rapier, Luther employed a cudgel. It was none the less a powerful piece of reasoning which led Erasmus to pen a ponderous and hostile reply. Luther then wrote an open letter, caustic as well as bitter, addressed to the 'viper' who had now revealed himself as an enemy of the truth. The clash, which made the two men into irreconcilable enemies, showed that there was a real difficulty in reconciling genuine humanism with dogmatic Protestantism.

This was not the only controversy in which Luther was involved in the 1520s. The early Evangelicals were agreed about certain fundamentals of which the most obvious were the repudiation of the Petrine theory and the necessary recognition of the Word of God as the basic authority of the Christian. In other matters there was room for wide divergence. In substituting the authority of the Word of God for that of the Church the Protestants ran into immediate trouble, since the claim that the Scriptures were self-authenticating was plainly shown to be full of difficulty. The early reformers were thus reduced to relying on individual interpretation. Münzer alone had made the arrogant claim that true believers were personally inspired by God and were so authorised to interpret the Scriptures. The reformers did however claim that the Word of God was plain and straightforward, at least as far as they and their followers were concerned, and they were not slow to believe that their enemies were inspired by the Devil. The elucidation of the Word of God provided abundant opportunity for the proliferation of sects.

The questions which confronted the reformers concerned the interpretation of the Mass, Communion, Lord's Supper, the Eucharist, the central liturgical act of the majority of the Christian believers. Luther's own view, as we have said earlier, was vigorous rather than precise. He had repudiated the scholastic theory of transubstantiation and with it the sacrificial interpretation of the Mass, by which the priest offers continually the sacrifice of Christ on the Cross. The Mass was for him a communion of believers; but he retained his belief that Christ was truly and really present in the sacrament, formulating the doctrine known as consubstantiation or, in Oecolampadius' word, impanation. In his *Confession concerning the Lord's Supper*, published in 1528, he asserted that sinful men can only commune with God through a sensible vehicle which they apprehend through faith; he held that Jesus Christ is the mediator of salvation and is present in the Eucharist as in his human and divine nature, in accordance with his own words 'This is my body' ('*Hoc est corpus meum*'). Christ is actually present to the believer, in Luther's words 'is bodily present and with whom the believer comes into actual contact—actually eats His flesh and drinks His blood and experiences the grace of forgiveness which it conveys'. His critics believed, perhaps rightly, that while Luther had discarded the scholastic interpretation of the Mass, he had retained the basic belief in inherent sacramental grace.

More radical reformers questioned the validity of Luther's interpretation. He expounded *Hoc est corpus meum* in a literal sense; but the meaning of the Eucharist was fundamentally changed if the phrase was understood spiritually or symbolically. The Dutch scholar, Cornelius Hoen, influenced by reading a tract on the Eucharist by Wessel Gansfort, a member of the Brethren of the Common Life, came to this conclusion. Christ's words must be interpreted figuratively not literally: 'is' really means 'represents' and was understood to accord with the Eucharistic discourse in the sixth chapter of St. John's Gospel. Meanwhile Luther's one-time colleague and now bitter enemy, Carlstadt, contended that the breaking of bread and the drinking of wine, were simply commemorative representations of the sacrifice on the Cross. 'This is my body which is given for you' referred not to the bread (though the previous phrase 'take, eat, &c' might well have landed him in an exegetical difficulty) but to the physical body of Christ. Carlstadt's exposition impressed the Strasbourg reformers, Bucer, Capito and others, who requested Luther (on November 23rd, 1524) to explain his position in this grave matter since their differences were only helping the common enemy. They asked him to deal with the situation dispassionately and without animus but this was unfortunately beyond Luther's power. 'The text is too mighty for me and will not be wrested from its sense in this fashion. . . . Carlstadt's vapourings have only led me to hold more strongly the opposite view.'

Erasm

From a portrait by Hans Holbe

32   John Frederick, Elector of Saxony
From a portrait by Titian

Titian painted the Elector's portrait while he was the Emperor's prisoner
Mühlberg, recovering from a cheek wound he had received there.

He trounced his fellow reformer soundly, belabouring him for resting his interpretation on Frau Hulda, the Devil's whore, his own reason, and in a passionately-argued discourse *Against the Heavenly Prophets* full of powerful dialectic, put forward his own view.

Now another disputant, more worthy of Luther's steel, made his appearance, the Swiss reformer Ulrich Zwingli. Born a native of canton Glarus, Zwingli had been early subject to humanist and Erasmian influences at the universities at which he studied, was then ordained a priest, but his study of the Scriptures led him to avow increasingly advanced views. He became the leader of Church reform in the prosperous lakeside town of Zürich in opposition to his diocesan, the Bishop of Constance. He acted in collaboration with the town council of Zürich in promoting reform, reforming the Mass, fostering clerical marriage (which enabled Zwingli to regularise an irregular union with Anna Reinhard) and serving the interests of Zürich (and other Swiss cantons in alliance with her) in attacking foreign influences and alliances. Zwingli certainly tended to identify the urban and economic imperialism of Zürich with the expansion of the reformed faith. He was no more ready than Luther to tolerate religious individualism; recalcitrant Anabaptists were drowned in the still waters of the Zürchersee.

On the face of it Zwingli seemed to have much in common with Luther, but they strongly disagreed over the interpretation of the Eucharist. Zwingli, influenced by Hoen, believed that it should be representational, that *est* meant *significat*; nor is the reception of the Lord's Supper essential to salvation (which depends on faith in the atoning death of Christ on the Cross). He expounded his views in 1525 in the tract *True and False Religion* which stimulated a bitter controversy in which Luther shrilly maintained that Zwingli and his fellow reformer, Oecolampadius, were under the influence of the Devil and that their teaching was no better than that of the papists. He could not wish for fellowship with such perverters of the Gospel; 'Cursed be such charity and such unity to the very bottom of hell, since such unity not only miserably disrupts Christianity, but makes sport and foolishness of it in a childish manner'.

But Luther's fellow reformers were somewhat less violent. Zwingli himself had greater respect for the German than Luther had for him. The cleavage only served the objects of their enemies whom the course of events seemed to be strengthening. The Lutheran princes, less concerned with the subtleties of Eucharistic theology, were especially worried by a recent decision promoted at the second Diet of

Speyer, and they felt that unity of action was vital for the defence, even the preservation of the evangelical cause. The masterful if impulsive Landgrave Philip of Hesse, supported by Elector John of Saxony, intervened in the academic debate and pressed the theologians to come together in conference at the castle of Marburg in October, 1529.

The conference consisted of all the leading reformers, Melanchthon, Justus Jonas, Oecolampadius, Bucer, Zwingli, Luther and many others. It lasted from October 1st to 3rd and showed the difficulty of reaching an agreement. The debates were erudite, frank and forceful. Luther was grimly uncompromising. 'The words *Hoc est corpus meum* are not ours, but Christ's', he declared, '*da kan der Teuffel nicht für*, the devil himself cannot make it otherwise. I ask you therefore to leave off your tampering with the Word and give glory to God.' 'And we', the Swiss reformer replied, 'ask you to give glory to God and leave off your quibbling.' Tempers ran so high that it seemed impossible to find a formula that would satisfy all parties. All that could be done was to salvage those points on which the reformers were in agreement. The 15 Articles of Marburg set out the chief doctrines of the reformed creed, and if momentarily this seemed but a small gain, yet it may have eventually prepared the way for the successful accord with the south German theologians forged at the Wittenberg Concordat of 1536.

The Conference at Marburg had been convoked at the initiative of the Landgrave Philip to enable the Protestants to meet a steadily deteriorating political situation. The previous five years had seen a hardening of opinion and the formation of leagues, Catholic and Pro-testant, to defend each other's territories and faith. The Catholic princes had come together under the lead of Duke George of Saxony and the Electors of Brandenburg and Mainz at Dessau in July, 1525; nearly a year later the Lutherans led by the Elector of Saxony and Philip of Hesse had formed a counter-league at Torgau. In the absence of the extreme anti-Lutheran group, the pro-Lutheran princes and the moderate Catholics had met together at the Diet of Speyer to pass a recess asserting that each prince 'is to live, govern, and bear himself as he hopes and trusts to answer to God and his Imperial majesty'. This attempt to provide for freedom of action was unlikely to succeed in the feverish religious situation. Another diet which foregathered at Speyer in 1529 was more fully representative of Cath-olic interests. It immediately reversed the recess promulgated in 1526 and forbade the Evangelicals to make any innovations in religion or to secularise ecclesiastical property. This decision led to the famous protestation signed by six princes and 14 imperial princes, which conferred the name Protestant on the reformers. They claimed that 'in matters which concern God's honour and salvation and the eternal life of our souls, everyone must stand and give account before God for himself'.

Moreover, the Emperor Charles V, momentarily freed by the Peace of Cambrai from Italian and French problems with which he had been grappling during the past few years, and once more on German soil after seven years' stay in Spain, was better placed than he had been for some time to impose the Edict of Worms. While many still believed that a reconciliation between Lutherans and Catholics was by no means impossible, the signs were ominous. The armed struggle, which Luther had so much hoped to avoid, seemed about to break out, and to begin with the reformed ranks still bitterly divided. That an uneasy peace in fact continued was by and large a result of Imperial policy and external issues.

CHAPTER 8

*Expansion and
the Search for a Religious
Compromise*
1529–1541

The failure to reach a concordat with the Swiss reformer, Zwingli,
and with the Protestants of the south German cities, and temporary
resurgence of Imperial power seemed doubly ominous for Luther and
his followers; but, in practice, in spite of the apparently dangerous
position in which German Protestant fortunes were placed by the
concatenation of these events, an uneasy truce continued to persist.
This was more the result of the complex pattern of Imperial politics
than the native strength of Lutheranism itself, though even Luther

was at last compelled to realise that the maintenance of his cause might necessitate the use of force. If political intrigue and religious discussion provided the background to his life at Wittenberg in the 1530s, it represented only a fraction of his existence.

The reformer was now deeply involved in domestic and family life. 'My Lord Katie greets you', he wrote in 1535 with reference to his wife, 'she plants our fields, pastures and sells cows et cetera. In between she has started to read the Bible. I have promised her 50 gulden if she finishes by Easter. She is hard at it and is at the end of the fifth book of Moses.' Children were born and had to be brought up. It is against such a background that Luther becomes a human, attractive character. He was occasionally irritated by the distractions of family and married life: 'Christ said we must become as little children to enter the kingdom', Luther commented in 1538, glancing at his family, the eldest of whom was 12, the youngest, 4, 'Dear God, this is too much. Have we got to become such fools?' But he could write in charming fashion to four-year-old Hans: 'I know a lovely garden where many children in golden jackets gather rosy apples under the trees, as well as pears, cherries, and yellow plums. They sing, skip and are gay. And they have pretty little ponies with golden bridles and silver saddles. I asked the gardener whose children they were, and he replied, "They are the children who like to pray and enjoy studying and be good." And I said, "Good man, I too have a son, whose name is Hans Luther. Couldn't he come into the garden, too, and eat the nice apples and the pears and ride a fine pony and play with these children?" And the man replied, "If he likes to pray and studies hard and is very good, he too may come into the garden, and Lippus and Jost [the children of the reformers Melanchthon and Jonas] can come with him; and when they all come together, they shall have golden whistles and drums and fine silver crossbows." . . . So, my darling son, study hard and pray well and tell Lippus and Jost to do this too, so that you may all come together into the garden.' Endowed with a delicate imagination and suffused by such feeling that he could weep over a violet drooping in the snow, Luther revealed tender affection as well as spiritual sensitivity once the shrill voice of the polemist was silenced. 'Good God', he would say, 'what a lot of vexation there is in marriage! Adam has made a muck of our nature. Think of all the rows Adam and Eve must have had in the course of their 900 years. Eve would say "You ate the apple", and Adam would reply,"You gave it to me".' But where would Luther have been without his precious Katie? He jokingly called her 'his Lord' and with his liking for puns turned

Katie into *Kette* (chain). 'Oh, Katie,' he told her when he was ill, 'do not die and leave me.' The marriage which had been founded on convenience ripened into affection. The older Luther became, and in his middle years he aged quickly, the more dependent he was on his wife to sustain him in his constant illnesses and depressions, the more the domestic background could cast into temporary oblivion the world and the Church.

He continued to be enormously industrious. He churned out controversial pamphlets attacking the Pope and the curia with almost hysterical passion. In 1537 he used the so-called Donation of Constantine (the pretended gift of the fourth-century Roman Emperor to the Pope of the western Empire shown to be a forgery in the fifteenth century by Nicholas of Cusa, Bishop Pecock and Lorenzo Valla) to charge the Pope with the ambition of Satan: 'From this it is perfectly plain how, out of the Papacy, founded on sheer lies and idolatry, has grown a real empire of Satan, to the destruction, not only of the Christian churches, but of the kingdoms of this world.' He pounded the curia with incessant virulence, loading his attacks with such vulgar abuse, occasionally in language anal and obscene, that his phrases concealed the measured criticism of a penetrating mind. The lesser lights within the Roman Church were given as short shrift. Duke George of Saxony, consistent at least in his constant opposition to his cousin's protégé, encouraged Luther's early admirer, but for long his bitter critic, Cochlaeus, to attack the reformer. Luther dismissed Cochlaeus as Dr. Gowk, 'the proper term to express his distinctive character', and flung down the gauntlet to Duke George and his fellow Catholic princes. 'When I pray I can only curse them. Shall I say "Hallowed be Thy name", I must add, "Cursed, damned, dishonoured be the name of the papists and all who blaspheme Thy name".' He added that he retained 'a good friendly, peaceful and Christian heart towards all men', but the evidence for this in his polemic writing was sadly lacking.

His old foe, the Archbishop of Mainz, who played a prominent part in forming a Catholic league of princes opposed to Luther, had expelled the Lutheran counsellors from the town of Halle. Luther was incited to catalogue the Archbishop's misdeeds by the publication of a collection of epigrams by a graduate of Wittenberg, Lemnius, who praised the Archbishop for his patronage of culture. The Saxon professor, furious at the treasonable sentiments of his former pupil, secured the prompt expulsion of the 'gutter poet' from Wittenberg, and attacked the Archbishop for his maladministration of justice (more especially the sentence of death which had been imposed on one of his own fiscal agents, von Schonitz, in 1535 for offences which had been in fact sponsored by his own government). The Archbishop, he declaimed, had all the vices that would justify his election as pope. In 1541 it was the turn of another Catholic prince, Duke Henry of Brunswick, whom he attacked as 'Hans Wurst' (Sausage).

He was, however, almost as vitriolic in criticising the left-wing Protestants, the Anabaptists who, radical in their political and social teaching, under the lead of two extraordinary fanatics, Jan Matthys and his disciple Jan Bockelson, had seized the town of Münster by violence in 1534. The new Jerusalem inaugurated at Münster with curious pageantry added the joys of polygamy to the pleasures of violence and social revolution before authority was restored by savage repression in 1536. The Anabaptists of Münster did not in fact represent the more moderate, quieter type of religious radical who was to be found among the urban proletariat of the Low Countries and south Germany. They constituted a significant third force in the Protestant Reformation, averse to the more conservative reformers' dependence on the support of the secular rulers, radical in their social thinking, inclined to pacifism, opposed to justification by faith, preferring to stress in its stead the experience of spiritual regeneration and the gift of the Holy Spirit. There was indeed a vast range in spirituality and in teaching, nor were the loosely interrelated groups ever in sight of unity; but they were all most equally condemned by the conservative reformers. Zwingli supported by the town council of Zürich had not hesitated to persecute. Luther, much alarmed at the increase in the number of their adherents (which his own support of the established order in the Peasants' War may well have served to stimulate) was at first content simply to repudiate their doctrines, more especially their insistence on adult baptism, founded on their belief that only the adult can experience the true spiritual regeneration or new birth which they regarded as a necessary antecedent to baptism. Indeed at first he had criticised the brutal treatment meted out to them by the German Catholics. 'I am very unwilling', he wrote in 1528, 'to sponsor the sentence of blood even when it is most justly deserved.' The appearance of Anabaptism in central Germany, and in Saxony in particular, made him much more vehement. 'As they are not only blasphemous, but highly seditious' he said in 1530, 'encourage the use of the sword against them by right of law. For it is in agreement with the will of God that he should be punished who ever resists the civil power as the minister of God.' The outbreak at Münster confirmed

his belief that the civil magistrates should proceed against the Anabaptists and like-minded radicals with the utmost severity and he
lamented the apparent leniency of some of his colleagues.

There was indeed no intermission in the need for polemic writing.
His former colleague, John Agricola of Eisleben, provoked his wrath
by stressing the antithetical qualities of the Law and the Gospel and
the comparative unimportance of the first by comparison with the
latter. Luther accused him with teaching antinomianism and ful-
minated with his pen and from the pulpit. Agricola and those who
supported him were hypocrites inspired by Satan. He was even
prepared to censure Melanchthon himself for his lack of strictness;
'You, Philip, are too indulgent towards the Antinomians, who have
openly proclaimed, "To the gallows with Moses". You ought rather
to help me, in pursuing them as enemies.' Eventually his 'perfidious
and abandoned' foe fled from Wittenberg where he had been detained,
pending an investigation by the Elector, to become court preacher to
the Elector of Brandenburg. The Swiss reformer, Zwingli, had been
killed in battle against the Catholic cantons some years previously (in
1531); but the theologians at Zürich continued to propagate his views.
Luther did not easily forgive their apparent independence of outlook
and attacked them as authors of subversion and blasphemy. 'I will',
he said in 1543, 'be no party to their perdition and their blasphemous
teaching, but remain guiltless and pray and teach against them to the
end of my days. God deliver the poor Church from such seducers.
Amen.'

Such was the extent of the controversy in which Luther was
absorbed, both within and without the reformed ranks, that it would
be easy to suppose that this was what took up the greater part of his
time and attention. The assumption would be manifestly unjust, for
in spite of constant acrimonious debate and in spite of the growing
gravity of the political situation the Lutheran Church was in a process
of formation under his direction, nor did he cease from his penetrating
theological studies.

The change-over from the Roman to Evangelical faith was not all
that easily effected. If the former church buildings could be easily
adapted to their new function—and under Luther's guidance the old
services were modified and Germanised to suit the doctrinal demands of
the new situation—numberless administrative problems still required
solution. With whom, for instance, was the final responsibility for
governing the Church, ordaining and selecting its minister? Who
controlled its endowments, secured its stipends and promoted its social

33   Peasants plundering a monastery
From Bainton, 'Here I Stand', Abingdon Press

and educational work? By whom and for what causes should ecclesiastical discipline be applied? All these problems required rethinking
if they were to be answered satisfactorily in the confused contemporary
atmosphere. Luther himself was naturally inundated with enquiries
from reformed churches, not merely in Saxony but from all over
Germany, as to what kind of constitution should be employed for their
governance and what forms of worship they should follow. If the
Roman Catholics sometimes thought of Luther as a kind of anti-pope,
even some of his followers occasionally felt that his position was
remotely, even dangerously, pontifical. 'You will never bring us
under a Pope', one of his colleagues warned him in February, 1532,
'we have become much too cunning for that.' Luther had, however,
no juridical authority in the Church; he was simply a private individual
whose pre-eminence had been achieved by his own genius. He did not,
however, always find it easy to correlate his standing in the movement with his lack of any effective authority.

   The organisation of the Reformed Church was in part a haphazard growth. Luther himself had to accommodate his theology to the needs of practical church politics. There was inevitably something opportunistic about the sequel. The ultimate authority of the Word of God depended on its interpreters, in practice the ministers, and those who were able to ensure its acceptance, in practice the civil magistrates. Logically Luther's adumbration of the priesthood of all believers might well have led him to place spiritual authority, the appointment of ministers and the control of church property in the hands of the congregation, or at least of the elect. This is what happened in some of the more radical reformed churches, and it seems highly probable that this constituted his ideal. His own knowledge of what happened in those places where the congregation had taken control and his implicit distrust of democratic procedure, all of which the threat of Anabaptism and his experience of the Peasants' War enhanced, made him rely effectively on the divinely-ordained civil magistrate. In his *Address to the German Nobility*, published in 1520, he had declared that the civil authority was responsible for reforming the Church. In 1526 he asked the Elector of Saxony to undertake the organisation of the Church in his territories, with the result that a Church Ordinance to that end was promulgated in 1527–8. The persistence of disorder led to a further appeal to the Elector in 1531. He was persuaded that a revision of the original instructions was necessary, both to safeguard ministers against ill-treatment by local authorities and to prevent the misappropriation of church revenue as well as to protect congregations against incompetent and corrupt ministers. The new Elector, John Frederick, issued revised Church Ordinances in 1532 for the regulation of Church life in Saxony.

These sets of ordinances provided for the government of the Reformed Church in the Electorate itself as well as for territories subject to the Elector's authority in Meissen and Voigtland, Thuringia and Franconia. Wittenberg was recognised as the ecclesiastical centre of Saxony. Its minister (who was to be assisted by four caplans or deacons and two preachers in the Castle Church) together with the provost of Kemberg were given the title of superintendents and supervisory charge over all the clergy. The city minister was to be elected by representatives of the university and town council. The ordinance approved daily and Sunday services in accordance with Luther's German Mass of 1526 and the previous ordinances of 1528. It also made provision for the instruction of the people and children according to Luther's catechism, the observance of the principal Christian festivals, the continuance of the practice of auricular confession, the education of children and the care of the sick and the poor. The ordinances of 1528 had laid down rules for the excommunication of unworthy members; but in the main the punishment of ecclesiastical offences and the maintenance of Christian morality were left to the civil magistrates and the civil courts, itself an indication of the close alignment that was to exist between the godly magistrate and the Reformed Church in Luther's State.

Although Luther did not doubt that the secular magistrate had a divine obligation to take responsibility for the organisation of the Church, his roots were too deeply entrenched in medieval thought for him to be a thoroughgoing Erastian. His attitude towards the relationship of the secular and spiritual powers, given the fact that the Pope had not been eliminated from the scene, was basically medieval. Ideally the Church as a spiritual body was a self-authenticating authority dependent only on the Word of God; the secular power was there to co-operate with it and to afford it support. In theory Luther was as much an exponent of the Gelasian separation of powers as any early medieval writer. He did not believe that the secular power should properly intervene in spiritual matters. But in practice the abolition of the sacerdotal and sacramental authority of the priesthood and of the ecclesiastical hierachy which ordained it left a vacuum which Luther was unwilling to fill by the congregation and which eventually placed him at the mercy of the godly prince. Thus it was the civil authority which drew up the ordinances for his Church and which, for instance, acted as arbitrator, at Luther's request, when there was at Zwickau in 1531 a dispute between the minister and the local authorities. This was not really what Luther wanted and he may have regarded the existing situation as a temporary expedient, but, like the dictatorship of the proletariat, it soon assumed permanence.

But what was the Christian's duty if the Prince proved to be ungodly? At first sight Luther might seem to have placed unqualified power in the hands of the civil magistrate. He certainly stressed his divinely-ordained authority and the Christian's responsibility to obey even the unjust monarch. 'The hand that wields the secular sword', he said in 1526, 'is not a human hand but the hand of God. It is God, not man, who hangs and breaks on the wheel, decapitates and flogs: it is God who wages war.' 'I will side always', he had written six years earlier, 'with him, however unjust, who endures rebellion and against him who rebels, however justly.' Consistency was not indeed Luther's strong point, but he would never have accepted the thesis that there were no limitations on the power of the secular magistrate.

For while he believed that the Prince was obliged to maintain the true religion, it was not his office to declare what the true religion was. When the Prince was acting as the protector of man-made law, the Christian was obliged to obey him; but the Christian was ultimately governed by the law of God expressed through the Scriptures and the law of nature, *natürlich Recht*, written in man's heart and conscience. 'Without love and natural justice you can never be in accord with the will of God, though you have devoured the jurists and all their works.' The Christian cannot be forced to contravene the law of God, and may because of his prior loyalty to it be obliged to disobey the civil magistrate. It is impossible to draw a fully coherent theory of political obligation from Luther's writings, in part because this was not his prior interest. Ideally law must give way to the spirit as force gives way to love; but in the imperfect Christian world in which he was living law and force were both necessary. Luther reluctantly recognised that this was so, and as he grew older and to some extent disillusioned he came to rely more and more on the support of the secular Prince; but he never wholly gave up the ideals which he had cherished as a younger man. In 1542 he consecrated an evangelical bishop for Naumburg, hoping thereby to establish a precedent for the government of the Church and to replace the temporary or emergency rule of the Prince.

Luther was happiest in his distinctively liturgical and theological work, in his hymns and devotional writings, since here at least he was free from the political and social factors which conditioned so much of what he did and gave to the Lutheran Reformation something of its opportunistic character.

In some sense the creation of the Lutheran Church took place under the continuous threat of war and repression. The situation in 1530 had favoured the Emperor Charles V to a greater extent that it had done since his accession 11 years earlier. He had made peace with Francis I of France at Cambrai the previous year. The slippery Medici pope, Clement VII, had been brought to heel at last and with an ill-grace carefully concealed (the Bishop of Tarbes noted that his Holiness 'when he thought no one saw him . . . heaved such sighs that heavy as his cope was, he made it shake in good earnest'), placed the Imperial crown on Charles' head at Bologna in February, 1530. In return Charles had promised that he would repress heresy in his dominions, by force if necessary. The Spanish revenues reinforced by the treasure of the New World were available to finance such projects as Charles might initiate in Germany, which he was visiting for the first time for nine years. After failing to take Vienna the previous year the Turks were temporarily quiet, and the Protestants, as we have seen, were much divided. Such a favourable situation was unlikely to last long, for the Valois king, thoroughly unreliable, and the Medici Pope, almost as untrustworthy, were equally opposed to the resurgence of Imperial fortunes.

Moreover the Emperor was not himself entirely clear in his own mind as to what was the right policy to adopt towards the Lutherans. Nine years previously, inexperienced and confident of his faith, he would readily have implemented the Edict of Worms if the princes had been willing to support him. Time, however, had taken its toll. The burdens of government had prematurely aged him. His prolonged contact with the Papacy had revealed a readiness to intrigue and an apparent worldliness on the part of the curia of which he had indeed greater personal experience than Luther himself. No shadow of doubt had weakened his strong if conventional faith; but he could not ignore the political implications of a repressive religious policy backed by force. He had no wish to alienate the growing body of Protestant princes and cities. There was an influential group of moderates, Erasmian in inclination, among them his former Chancellor, Mercurino Gattinara, who believed in the possibility of compromise. Later on Charles' instructions, Cornelius Schepper consulted the Bishop of Augsburg, Christopher von Stadion, who submitted a number of points for the Emperor's consideration. Many of these went far to meet Lutheran objections on points of doctrine. He warned the Emperor that Lutheranism could not be suppressed by force. The Emperor had himself become convinced that a General Council of reform was a first necessity if the Protestants were to be conciliated. At worst, it might be advisable to call a purely German council. There was thus a strong third party with adherents on both sides which was reluctant to press matters to an extreme conclusion. Even Luther was ready to consider the possibility, though he thought that there was little chance of genuine accommodation. Some of his colleagues, Melanchthon in particular, were more hopeful. When, therefore, Charles crossed the Alps in the summer of 1530, in spite of pressure from Cardinal Campeggio who accompanied him, he issued a summons to the Diet at Augsburg which was sweetly moderate in its tone.

He was, however, only too soon confronted by the difficulties implicit in the situation, as the letter which he wrote to his wife, the Empress Isabella, on July 8th, 1530 clearly shows: 'I came through Bavaria, where the Dukes, my true friends and servants, received me well. I entered Augsburg on the vigil of Corpus Christi (June 16th) and was solemnly received by Electors, princes and ambassadors. On the following day they held the procession which had been discontinued for some years. I took part in it as usual. And, although some of the Lutherans refused to participate, I had a good following, for those who stand firm in the faith outnumber by many those who do not. We have already started on the religious question and are tearing out heresy by the roots. Far the most dangerous people in this town are the chaplains of the Lutheran princes. Therefore I have proclaimed that, under penalty, no one shall preach who has not been selected by me. This proclamation was unanimously accepted. This is a good beginning.' In the sermon which he preached at the opening of the Diet, Cardinal Pimpinelli exhorted Charles to employ the sword of St. Paul against the heretics who had scorned the keys of St. Peter.

The moderates strove for mastery in the warm summer days. In the hope of providing material which might help towards a settlement, Melanchthon and some of his fellow theologians submitted a document, a Confession of Faith, for the consideration of the Emperor and the Diet which was designed to prove the orthodoxy of the Lutheran position and to refute the oft-repeated charges that they were heretics such as those who had been rightly condemned by the Church in earlier ages. They were shown to hold the Catholic belief in relation to the Trinity, the redemptive work of Christ and the sacraments; they accepted the Real Presence of Christ in the Eucharist, the proper use of confession, penitence and absolution. Yet equally they stated, though in temperate fashion, their belief in the doctrine of justification by faith and the Lutheran view of the Church. The second part of the Confession consisted of a full statement of contemporary abuses and a demand for communion in both kinds and clerical marriage. It implicitly made plain the dividing line between Lutheran teaching and that of the Zwinglians and the Anabaptists (whom the Confession condemned), so much so that only two of the German cities that had signed the original Protestation of Speyer, Nuremberg and Reutlingen, were ready to accept the Confession.

The document was a moderate, even a liberal statement, but it had relatively little chance of acceptance. It left too much unsaid. It skated over vital issues, the number of the sacraments, the meaning of the Eucharist and the authority of the Papacy. If Melanchthon had been ready to sacrifice the potential unity of the Protestant party to avoid assimilating the theologically unacceptable views of Zwingli and the south German Evangelicals, he had not gone far enough to win the Catholic partisans. Luther, who had no personal part in drawing up the Confession and for obvious reasons was not at Augsburg, had given the document a somewhat hesitant approval when he had received it at the castle of Coburg where he was laid low by insomnia and nervous prostration; but he was pessimistic. It was soon clear that his fears were justified. Melanchthon was as conciliatory as he could be in discussions with the papal legate but neither Campeggio, who was acting under direct instructions from Rome, nor the more forthright members of the Catholic party, like Duke George of Saxony, were ready for any concessions. They were for an abrupt repudiation of the Confession, but the more moderate Catholics headed by the Archbishop of Mainz advised a presentation of a Confutation of the Confession before the Emperor demanded the submission of the Lutherans. Great care was taken in drawing up the Confutation nor was it intemperate in its statements; but it underlined the difficulty of reaching any agreed solution. The Emperor, who had taken a personal interest in its composition, eventually agreed to accept it and once more avowed his readiness to enforce the true faith by force if necessary. Landgrave Philip of Hesse, believing that no further good could come from discussion, left the city abruptly without taking the leave of the Emperor. But Charles V was not yet ready to push matters to extremities. He still believed that a council was the only practical answer to the religious difficulties, and he brought as much pressure as he possibly could on the reluctant Pope. 'If there were to be no council', he warned Clement VII, 'Germany, the strongest and most warlike nation in Christendom, would fall into the most serious danger. At present the world is at peace so that a council can easily be called to prevent the further breeding of schism. . . . Therefore I entreat and beseech you to consent to the council, so that we may avoid the burden of blame and win the approval of all good men.' Clement, however, remained adamant in his opposition. The Emperor was himself concerned with winning the help of the princes against the Turks and securing his brother Ferdinand's election as King of the Romans. Thus encouraged by his comparatively conciliatory attitude, Melanchthon plunged once more into discussion, making concessions which alarmed some of his less pliant colleagues.

Among them was Luther, who had concluded that there was no real hope of compromise and was anxious lest the basic fundamentals of the Protestant faith should be weakened, thus having an adverse effect on the Evangelical cause. 'Be careful', he told Melanchthon on August 26th, 1530, 'that you do not give more than you have, so that we may not be driven anew to a more arduous and dangerous struggle in defence of the Gospel. . . . In brief, this negotiation for a doctrinal agreement is altogether displeasing to me. It is to attempt the impossible unless the Pope is willing to abolish his Papacy.' His attitude was refreshingly realistic. 'I hear', he wrote to Spalatin, 'that, albeit not willingly, you have begun a wonderful work at Augsburg, viz., that of uniting the Pope and Luther. But the Pope will not, and Luther declines.'

The Emperor had by now reached a similar conclusion. On September 22nd, 1530, he presented a recess to the Diet, declaring that the Confession had been refuted and declaring that the articles set out in the Confutation must be accepted within six months pending the meeting of a General Council of the Church. The Elector's chancellor on behalf of the signatories of the Confession declared that they could not comply with the recess. The cleavage was confirmed by subsequent discussions; and the representatives of the Protestant estates gradually left Augsburg. A Catholic rump cheered the edict with which the Emperor closed the Diet on November 19th, 1530, reaffirming the decision promulgated at Worms. 'This doctrine', it asserted, 'which has been already condemned, has given rise to much misleading error among the common people. They have lost all true reverence, all Christian honour; discipline, fear of God and charity to their neighbour—these are utterly forgotten.'

The stage might well have been set for the outbreak of religious war, since the only possible appeal seemed to be to naked force, but in fact nothing happened. There was, however, a steady hardening of opinion among the Protestant princes who felt that a time had come to form a defensive military alliance which was in fact negotiated at meetings at Schmalkalden in December, 1530 and February, 1531. As a result of Bucer's mediation the principal south German cities, Magdeburg, Bremen, Strasbourg, Ulm, Constance, Reutlingen, Memmingen, Isny, Biberach and Lindau, were brought into alliance with the leading Lutheran princes, Elector John of Saxony, Landgrave Philip of Hesse, Duke Ernest of Lüneburg, Philip of Grubenhagen, the Count of Mansfeld and the Prince of Anhalt. Luther, who held Charles V in great respect in spite of his occasional angry sallies, was at first reluctant to sponsor a possible policy of resistance to Imperial authority, but he was at last convinced by the Saxon jurists that the Word of God must be defended and that if they were obliged to fight, they would not be fighting against the Emperor but the Pope and the Romanists who had deceived him. 'If the Emperor shall declare war in the Pope's behalf, or on account of our teaching, let no one abet his purpose or show him obedience, but be assured that God utterly forbids him to obey his mandate. Whoever yields obedience for such a purpose is disobedient to God and shall lose both body and soul in such a war. For the Emperor in this matter acts not only against God and His Divine law, but against his own Imperial law, oaths, and obligations.'

Much to Luther's relief, for he believed that force did not solve any problem, the Schmalkaldic League was not yet obliged to resort to force. Its diplomatic manœuvrings, combined with the kaleidoscopic pattern of German politics, proved sufficient to frustrate the Emperor's declared intention of implementing the Edict of Worms. The Elector and Philip of Hesse worked together to secure friendly support from the Catholic King of France and the Protestant King of England. They were moreover able to win over the Catholic Dukes Lewis and William of Bavaria, who were much opposed to the election of Ferdinand as King of the Romans. The opposition to the Emperor thus cut across political and religious divisions. Charles wrote gloomily to his wife about the deteriorating situation in July, 1531: 'I have had to postpone some of my plans for this year, for I had hoped that some decision about a Council might be reached, since the weal of Christendom hangs on it. But the Pope and the Most Christian King are still making difficulties which imperil the whole business. The postponement of the Council has had the worst effect in Germany. The Turkish menace has increased so much that I have even considered coming to an agreement with the Lutherans in order to prevent worse disaster.' The revival of the Turkish threat so alarmed the Emperor that he was obliged to come to terms with the Protestant princes who were not averse to exploiting the situation. When the Diet met at Nuremberg a religious peace was patched up; Charles promised to suspend proceedings against the Protestants in the *Reichskammergericht* over the secularisation of church property and to seek to ensure a meeting of the projected General Council within six months.

The comparative success of the Schmalkaldic League strengthened the Lutheran cause. The Turks had indeed retreated from the little fortress of Güns and Charles was given a triumphal entry into Vienna; but the Imperial cause suffered a defeat in another quarter. Philip of Hesse made contact with Francis of France, met him at Bar-le-Duc, and with some of the other anti-Hapsburg princes managed to secure the return to his Duchy of the unattractive, immoral Lutheran sympathiser, Ulrich of Wurttemberg, whose territory had been seized by Charles' brother, Ferdinand. In the subsequent Peace of Kaaden, signed in June, 1534, Ferdinand promised to suspend all prosecutions for religion against members of the league before the *Reichskammergericht*. The loss of Wurttemberg was strategically significant as the Duchy formed the connecting link between Hapsburg estates in the Tyrol, the Franche Comté and Alsace. The Lutherans were further emboldened by new accessions to the League, Wurttemberg, Pomerania, Anhalt, Augsburg, Frankfort, Hanover, Kempten and, between 1537 and 1539, Christian III of Denmark into whose territory Lutheran teaching had penetrated. The League entered into friendly negotiations with Henry VIII of England, who showed some interest in a projected union of Lutherans and Anglicans. There were overtures to Francis I of France, who actually invited Melanchthon to the French court to discuss the religious situation, an invitation he did not accept; and the south German towns were critical of an understanding with a king who, as the municipal council of Ulm put it, 'persecuted, tormented and hunted his own subjects out of house and home for the sake of God's word, and appalling to relate, had actually entered into alliance with the common foe of all good Christians, the Turk'.

A new turn to the religious situation was given by the election in 1534 of the Farnese pope, Paul III, who was at first genuinely anxious to convoke a General Council of the Church. He sent a nuncio to Germany, Paolo Vergerio, who had long conversations among others with Luther in November, 1535 (and who was incidentally eventually to become a Lutheran himself). Although the Lutherans had long been demanding a General Council, it was by no means clear that they would accept its recommendations. While Luther himself praised the idea of a 'free Christian General Council', he declared that the Reformed Church, relying on the Word of God, had already achieved what a General Council should set out to accomplish. 'I acted the real Luther throughout at the late interview', he told Jonas, 'and addressed the legate in the most disconcerting terms.' Luther had indeed few illusions about the deep cleavage which existed. He would have seen the point raised by the Catholic scholars, Nausea and Cochlaeus, when they asked: 'How can we hope to come to terms with people who regard the chief shepherd of Christ's flock as Antichrist? who ask us to accept the *Confessio Augustana*, an act that would be equivalent to apostasy from the Roman Catholic Church and throwing in our lot with them?'

Although Luther's uncompromising attitude could hardly be

regarded as representative, even of the Lutheran princes, Vergerio's early optimism soon ebbed. It was one thing to call a Council and yet another to ensure that there would be agreement about the nature of its authority or about the place where it was to meet. The Protestants wanted a Free Council, preferably in Germany with papal authority as far as possible excluded; but a consensus of Catholic opinion at last grudgingly agreed that Mantua, a fief of the Empire in Italy, was an acceptable venue. Preparations were put in train for the opening of a General Council there in 1537. This, however, never came to pass, in part because the Duke of Mantua had not been told early enough of the intention to make his capital city the scene of such a conference; when he learned what had been proposed he made impossible conditions as to the size of a papal 'police' force necessary for maintaining order. Had the Pope been in a position to supply such an army, which he was not able to do, there would have been some grounds for the constant Protestant assertion that such a Council was not wholly free.

In fact the Schmalkaldic League had already made known its disapproval of the intended Council. Its members would willingly participate in a Council 'in German lands', but since the Pope refused to submit to the authority of such a Council there was no guarantee that the Protestant participants would be free to come and go or that decisions reached were not dictated by the Pope. Subsequently opinion hardened, and after an unsatisfactory series of interviews with the Elector and others of the princes, in February, 1537, the papal legate, Peter van der Vorst, was left in no doubt as to their hostility. Luther was not himself present, as he was ill, but at the Elector's request he, helped by Melanchthon and some other theologians, drew up a list of doctrines which it was essential for the Lutherans to maintain. These *Schmalkaldic Articles*, if more generous in their final form than Luther had intended, showed the basic difficulty of reaching an accord without agreement as to the divine authority of the Pope. The Protestant princes declared flatly that the promised Council could not be regarded as the Free Christian Council in Germany demanded by the Estates and promised by Charles. 'We are unable to alter our view of the Pope's intentions and to accept the Council since acceptance would be the same as submitting in advance to the verdict which will surely be pronounced.' 'The freedom of the Council', they further declared, 'does not consist in the possibility of a free expression of opinion but in the Pope being debarred from the presidency. By a Christian Council we mean one whose only standard is Holy Scripture. . . . The Diet's demand for a German locality for

179

the Council conforms to the practice of the ancient Church. . . . We are not going to walk into the Pope's trap; for us Mantua is unacceptable.'

The chief responsibility for the failure of the Council to materialise at Mantua lay, however, neither with the Duke nor the Lutheran princes but with Francis I of France. The French king supposed that the Pope's plan for summoning a Council was first and foremost a plan to sponsor the Emperor's attempt to crush the Lutherans and secondly to avenge himself on Henry VIII of England for the insult that the latter had offered to his aunt, Catherine of Aragon. Francis was absolutely opposed to any measure that seemed to increase his adversary's power. He intimated that he would be ready to accept a Council, providing it was genuinely universal and held at a place outside the Emperor's sphere of influence; and he at once entered into negotiations with the Schmalkaldic League and anti-Hapsburg Catholic German princes.

The repercussions of the failure at Mantua, and an abortive attempt to arrange a Council at Vicenza, were Europe-wide and most pronounced in Germany, where the Catholic as well as the Protestant princes came to believe, albeit undeservedly, that Paul III was as insincere as his predecessor. The papal nuncios wrote gloomily about the increasingly desperate situation in Germany. Van der Vorst and Morone both insisted that unless a General Council was summoned the Catholics in Germany would be forced to accept a National Council. 'If the General Council does not meet', Morone wrote, 'there will be great upheavals in Germany.' Lutheran power increased steadily. The new Duke of Saxony, Henry, deserted his predecessor's faith. The new Elector of Brandenburg, Joachim II, influenced by his mother, inclined to the Lutheran cause. Some of the ecclesiastical princes were secularising their dioceses. All the Imperial cities in the south, including Augsburg, had turned Protestant. A crop of satires, including Luther's own vicious attack on the Pope in the tract on the Donation of Constantine, lampooned the council. 'If there is no Council', John Eck wrote to Cardinal Aleander, 'then woe to England! woe to Denmark, Sweden and Norway! When will the apostasy end?' The Catholic Federation of Nuremberg, of which the Vice-Chancellor, Matthias Held, had had high hopes, seemed dormant.

In fact the Pope's position was a very difficult one. If he was to call a Council, he must have the co-operation of the French; but Francis I suspected that a Council would increase the power of his enemy, the Emperor. On the other hand, Charles V believed that the Pope ought to abandon the neutral stand that he had adopted in the Hapsburg–Valois struggle and to sponsor the Hapsburg cause, preparatory to the calling of a Council and the suppression of heresy. Thus while the Pope was still eager to summon a Council (but not to concede an iota to the Protestants), there was an inevitable series of delays, arising from diplomatic and political rather than religious considerations.

It was at this juncture that Charles' brother Ferdinand, who was more in contact with German affairs, came, at the suggestion of Joachim II of Brandenburg, to the conclusion that one further attempt should be made to promote a reconciliation of the conflicting faiths. 'The Protestants', Joachim argued, 'will never send their representatives to the Council. They will be condemned, therefore, in their absence; they will accordingly offer armed resistance to the execution of its decisions; this means the dreaded war of religion. Should not yet another effort be made before the Council to bring about a friendly understanding with them—of course with the co-operation of papal commissaries?' The proposal met with a warm welcome in many quarters. While the Emperor had recently concluded a 10-year truce with France (in 1538), there were signs that the Turkish War was about to be renewed. Many Catholics believed that it was more expedient to encourage plans for a reconciliation with the Lutherans than to sponsor a Council which the majority of the Lutherans would probably boycott and which would give rise to a policy of repression likely to foster the power of the Emperor. Others genuinely believed that compromise was still possible. The Elector of Brandenburg, theologically naive, had sought to retain many Catholic practices together with Lutheranism in the Church Order which he had issued in 1540, and he was to attend Mass during the Diet of Ratisbon the next year. Even the Pope gave a reluctant consent to the promised conference which was attended by the diligent and intelligent Contarini as legate. He, however, no more than Luther himself, can have had much hope of any real agreement. Negotiations were, however, opened with the Schmalkaldic League at Frankfort in 1539, resulting in the Respite of Frankfort by which the members of the League agreed to send representatives to a Diet of princes to help finance the Turkish War in return for a suspension for some 15 months of suits against the Protestant princes in the Imperial Supreme Court.

The way was now clear for the colloquy at Ratisbon. Early in 1541 the redoubtable Eck and the scholarly Melanchthon met at Worms to debate the Confession of Augsburg as Melanchthon had now amended it. They found somewhat to their surprise that they both held the same

181

34   Ratisbon. *From Schedel, 'Weltchronik', 1493*

views about original sin, but before the discussion was further advanced the Emperor's representative adjourned the debate to the Diet which he had summoned to Ratisbon. The Emperor was there to open it in person in April, 1541; but in spite of his sincerity and the genuinely conciliatory language that he used the promise of any real treaty was slim. He himself had indeed recently initiated a policy of persecution against the Protestants in the Low Countries. Hopes of conciliation were raised by the adhesion (for completely personal and discreditable reasons) of the able and hitherto uncompromising Philip of Hesse to the moderate party. Bucer and Melanchthon were both optimistic, though Luther had impressed the latter that he must stand by the Confession of Augsburg. A delegate who attracted little attention at the time was John Calvin from Strasbourg.

Some progress was undoubtedly made before a sign of the genuine impasse appeared. Agreement was reached on the first four articles of the Book of Ratisbon, and on May 2nd, 1541, Lutherans accepted the fifth article, which maintained that justification is by faith working through charity. It was soon, however, clear that they could not accept either the sacramental nature of the Church or her sacramental constitution. The final break occurred over a discussion about the Eucharist, for Contarini would not permit any deviation from the recognised theory of transubstantiation.

The result did not surprise Luther. Neither he nor the Elector of Saxony had been present at Ratisbon. 'We hold', Luther wrote to the Elector, 'that man is justified by faith without the works of the law; this is our formula, and to this we adhere. It is short and clear. Let the devil and Eck, and whoever will, storm against it.' In a curious attempt to break the deadlock, the Elector of Brandenburg suggested to the Emperor that an appeal should be made to Luther himself. Although his reply was more conciliatory than could well have been hoped, he showed that he had no real confidence in the possibility of reaching an agreed solution. The Diet broke up after it had confirmed the Recess of Augsburg and its subsequent modification at the Diet of Nuremberg in 1532. All that could in fact be said was that the expected hostilities still hung fire. 'Was the war for which the firebrands were agitating really unavoidable?' the Imperial counsellor, Granvella, asked the papal legate, Morone, on May 28th, 1541, 'or should they be content with partial accord and tolerate the articles not yet agreed upon until the Council met?'

In remote Wittenberg Luther found the course of events depressing and exasperating He was so often ill. His nerves were frayed and his spirits low. Although he was held in the greatest esteem, his practical influence had faded in a quite remarkable way. When the Princess Elizabeth of Brandenburg, whom he had visited at Lichtenburg in June, 1539, wished him 40 years more of life, he replied characteristically that the world was so wicked that he could wish 'for nothing better than one blessed hour and then departure to the next'. 'I appear to myself a cold and useless corpse', he wrote in 1541, 'for which a sepulchre is the only fitting habitation.'

CHAPTER 9

The Last Years

1541–1546

By the 1540s Luther was beginning to fail. Professor, family man, theologian, he had seen his movement caught and inextricably held in the fine cobweb of European politics. He was personally averse to such development, but there was little that he could do about it. Indeed his influence had much diminished. He did not believe that the religious question could be effectively solved by the use of force and he did not approve of the strange bed fellows, the Catholic Francis I of France and the Moslem Sultan, Suleiman, with whom the princes of the Schmalkaldic League had to be metaphorically intimate. Indeed he held that the very dependence upon the princes which circumstances had forced upon Luther and the Evangelical Church was a manifest disadvantage.

This was in some respects illustrated by the notorious case of the Landgrave Philip of Hesse. The private lives of many of the German princes were a curious commentary on the Evangelical faith which they had, sincerely as it would seem, embraced; outwardly it appeared that they hoped to be justified by their faith rather than by their works. The reformers, who must have been aware of what was happening, just as Cranmer knew only too well of the moral vagaries of Henry VIII, were too dependent on their patronage, too much in awe of civil authority, to administer the kind of rebuke which, for instance, St. Boniface centuries ago had readily imparted to the Mercian kings. The two leading Lutheran princes were John Frederick, Elector of Saxony, and Philip, the Landgrave of Hesse. John Frederick was occasionally tipsy; Philip of Hesse had a very irregular sex life, as his wife, a Saxon princess, very well knew. By 1539 this syphilitic Evangelical had decided that the most effective method of discouraging the habit of fornication was to enter into a bigamous union, which would, he argued, satisfy the lusts of the flesh and yet give a kind of moral stability so far conspicuously lacking from his private life. The precocious young man had raised the issue of bigamy with Luther as early as 1526. Luther had naturally answered that a Christian could have no more than one wife, but he had made the curious reservation that certain circumstances, such as having a wife afflicted with leprosy, could conceivably justify a bigamous union. Thirteen years later, perhaps genuinely in love with Margaret von der Saale, Philip of Hesse approached Martin Bucer, who was sufficiently impressed by the polygamous behaviour of the patriarchs in the Old Testament to give his reluctant approval on the grounds that at least a bigamous marriage would eliminate the sin of fornication. He did, however, add that such a union must be kept absolutely secret. Bucer then consulted Luther and Melanchthon at Wittenberg. They came to a similar conclusion founded on the sexual customs of the Old Testament patriarchs, drawing up a declaration on December 10th, 1539, which gave virtual permission to Philip to go ahead with his projected union. While asserting that monogamy is the universal divine law, they agreed that polygamy had been conceded by God to the patriarchs because of the weakness of the flesh. They deprecated the irregular sex life of Philip of Hesse, reminded him that he ought to resist the lusts of the flesh according to the precepts of the Gospel and then, admitting though regretting his inability to remain continent, approved the bigamous union provided it was kept a strict secret. Acceptance of the document bristled with obvious difficulties, quite apart from the fact that if the union was to be kept a secret then Philip was giving the outside world a splendid example of fornication. Either the reformers were extremely confused and unduly influenced by the example of the Old Testament, which would seem unlikely in view of their high intelligence, or they were prompted to act as they did for reasons of political and religious expediency. Philip of Hesse was the founder and upholder of the Schmalkaldic League; the reformers were unready to disown a man of such noted military reputation whose defection would be a severe blow to their cause.

Luther and his colleagues had been surprisingly naive, more especially in their belief that the bigamous union could be kept secret. The 'marriage' had been performed by Philip's court chaplain, Melander, on March 4th, 1540, in the presence of Bucer, Melanchthon and others. It soon became widely known. Philip's sister, the Duchess of Rocklitz, in whose service Margaret had been, was extremely angry; the rightful Landgravine's uncle, the Duke of Saxony, was naturally furious. The scandal, as the reformers soon realised, was bound to do their cause a grave disservice. Philip of Hesse pressed for a public statement, but Luther robustly opposed this, preferring, as he bluntly put it, a 'good strong lie'. Feeling the cold wind of Evangelical disapproval, Philip moved steadily towards the Imperialists, persuaded that the Emperor could give him immunity from the consequences of his bigamous union.

The political scene was by and large increasingly gloomy, for the Diet of Ratisbon had shown how difficult it was to reach an agreeable solution, even under the most favourable circumstances and with the best will in the world. Charles V was soon involved in war with Francis I and with an expensive but unsuccessful expedition against Algiers; but the deterioration in Imperial fortunes did not last long. Many Germans, among them some Lutherans, were justifiably suspicious of the integrity of the French king, more especially after the Duke of Orleans had applied in the autumn of 1543 for membership of the Schmalkaldic League. The Imperial diplomats managed to negotiate a limited understanding with Henry VIII of England, and Charles' army at last pushed the French back towards their northern frontiers. The new Elector Palatine, though hardly consistent in his allegiance, had been connected to Charles V through his marriage to the Emperor's 14-year-old niece, Dorothea of Denmark. Philip of Hesse, smarting under the barrage of political disapproval, more definitely became Charles' man. At the Diet of Speyer, which lasted from February to June, 1544, Charles felt strong enough to advise mutual toleration and to promise both the calling of a General Council at least in Germany and a 'Christian Reformation', in return for which the Estates helped him against France and promised assistance against the Turks. New military successes forced Francis to sign the Treaty of Crépy in September, 1544.

Since fortune's wheel had once more turned in his favour, Charles was now better placed than for some years to deal with the disunion of the Church in Germany. Was he to implement the decisions which he had made recently at Speyer, proceed to a Christian reformation and the calling of a Council? Circumstances had, however, been some-what changed by Paul III's decision, hastened by the events at Speyer, to convoke a General Council of the Church to meet at Trent on March 15th, 1545. It was a clever move since it obviously made it much more difficult for the Emperor to carry out the projected Christian Reforma-tion. Effectively the decision to summon the Council of Trent broke the understanding between the Catholics and Protestants reached at Speyer. The Pope brought as much pressure as he could on the Emperor, sending Cardinal Farnese to promise financial help against the Turks—and the Protestants. Charles undoubtedly had misgivings about the renewal of the policy of repression. His sister, Mary of Hungary, who was regent of the Netherlands, always favourably inclined towards the Protestants, sought to dissuade him. Protestant opinion, hardened by rumours of the *rapprochement* between the Emperor and the Pope, still insisted that the decisions reached at Speyer should be implemented. Meanwhile the Catholic cause had been greatly strengthened by the adhesion of the young Duke Maurice of Saxony, who had quarrelled with his cousin, the Elector of Saxony, over the disposal of secularised church lands, and of two of the Bran-denburg princes, Hans of Brandenburg-Kustrin and Albert-Alcibiades of Brandenburg-Kulmbach, as well as by a reconciliation with the Catholic Duke of Bavaria. Each side took active measures to prepare for open war. In June, 1546, the Emperor signed a treaty of alliance with the Pope against the Protestants. The moment which Luther had so much dreaded had arrived; but the reformer was already dead.

In truth his powers were in some respects failing. The long proces-sion of illnesses weakened his constitution; nervous depression lowered his spirits. As his blood-pressure increased, his temper became more frayed. He was more and more irascible, not merely in controversy but in his ordinary day-to-day relations. His mind was as clear as ever, pungent, penetrating in its judgment, but his attacks on his critics were even more abusive, vulgar and hysterical than they had been.

188

Nor was he much encouraged by the progress of the Reformation. He had never taken kindly to the Zwinglians and would have no more to do with them now than in his earlier years. He scorned and attacked furiously Protestant radicals like Kaspar Schwenkfeld and Francke who did not accept that Luther's word was necessarily the Word of God. 'I can do no more here', he told Bugenhagen in November, 1545. 'The weariness of life', to which the death of his beloved daughter, Magdalena, in 1542, had much contributed, 'and the misery of my maladies' combined to fill him with foreboding. 'I am', he told Jacob Probst, 'exhausted with age and work—old, cold, and all out of shape—and yet I am not allowed to rest, but daily tormented with all manner of business and the toil of scribbling.'

The body was weak but the mind was clear and the spirit often serene. He felt, however, that he had grown out of sympathy with his times. Like old men in all ages, he deplored gloomily the morals and manners of the young. 'Everywhere', he wrote in April, 1543, 'the licence and impudence of the people increase. The magistrates are to blame, for they do nothing except exact taxes. The governments have become institutions for the ingathering of treasures and taxes. Therefore the Lord will destroy us in His anger. Would that the day of our redemption would quickly come!' New fashions and amusements in his own town made him consider seriously whether he should not leave Wittenberg; in the summer of 1545 he besought Katie to sell his house and gardens there so that they could retire to their small farm at Zulsdorf. The Elector and the town council promised to institute measures to enforce morality, and Luther came back to Wittenberg in mid-August, exhausted physically and mentally.

But he was sufficiently strong-willed to arrange a journey in the cold new year to act as an arbitrator between the counts of Mansfeld. Shortly before he left he wrote another letter to his friend Jacob Probst: 'Old, decrepit, bereft of energy, weary, cold, and now one-eyed I had hoped that now at least peace would be vouchsaved to me as to a dead man. And yet, as if I had never done anything, never spoken, written, achieved anything, I must still be overwhelmed with such toils. But Christ is all in all, both to do and to finish, blessed for ever!' He had not now long to wait. At Eisleben where he was staying his spirits revived and he preached to full churches and negotiated a satisfactory settlement; but the very same evening, February 17th, 1546, he had a heart attack and died at three o'clock the next morning. Four days later his body was buried at Wittenberg in the presence of a packed congregation in that Castle Church with

189

which his life had been so long, so eventfully and so intimately connected.

His death had few immediate repercussions as Lutherans and Catholics prepared for war. The desultory campaigns culminated in Charles' victory at Mühlberg on April 24th, 1547; the Elector, John Frederick, became his prisoner, as did eventually Philip of Hesse who had abandoned his Imperial master inexpediently in the middle of campaigning. Charles' military triumph did not, however, bring about any real solution. The General Council had met at Trent, but in May, 1547, to Charles' intense indignation, Pope Paul III moved it out of Imperial influence to Bologna; once more the Emperor talked of summoning a Council on his own initiative and of reforming the Church. These anti-papal moves at least commended him to the Protestants whom he was, for all his victory, powerless to suppress. On June 30th, 1548, he issued the *Interim*, designed to provide a temporary settlement along the lines of *cujus regio ejus religio*, that is, people must follow the faith of their sovereign, until a General Council achieved a settlement. Although much criticised and little observed, the *Interim* had the merit of preserving an uneasy peace. The death of Paul III and the accession of Julius III paved the way for the return of the Council of Trent; but Charles was too involved in war with Henry II of France, who had managed by the Treaty of Chambord to secure the help of the German Protestants (now led by Maurice of Saxony), to pay very much attention to the problem of religious conciliation. Prematurely aged, stricken with gout, disillusioned and tired, Charles was obliged to come to terms with his adversary and by the treaty of Passau in 1552 he recognised that Protestantism should be regarded as on the same footing as Catholicism, and that each prince should determine whether his subjects were to be Catholic or Lutheran. This settlement anticipated the final step which was taken at the Diet of Augsburg in 1555 by which the *cujus regio ejus religio* principle was made legally definitive. But by then Charles was only Emperor in name. He began to surrender his dignities so as to spend the remaining years of his life in a house close to the Hieronymite monastery at Yuste in Spain, not entirely without his creature comforts, but at least with the spiritual consolations of the religious faith to which he had been so loyally attached throughout his life.

It is possible that if Luther had been alive, he might have approved the settlement reached at Augsburg; though he would not very readily have tolerated the co-existence of the old religion. In fact the settlement and its aftermath amply illustrate the paradox of Luther's own position. He had been forced by circumstances to depend upon the civil magistrates; the decisions reached at Augsburg in 1555, which provided plenty of material for future disturbances, crystallised the Erastian character of the Lutheran Church. Its dependence upon the State moulded its history for the next four centuries and even in the twentieth century did much to condition the readiness with which it accepted the religious policy of Hitler and his associates. Fundamentally, however, Luther would only have accepted this as a temporary expedient. He was indeed ill-equipped as a politician and his ideas about authority were basically conservative and confused. But he knew none the less that the authority of the godly prince, much approved as it was in the Old Testament, itself depended ultimately upon its conformity with the law of God diffused through the Scriptures and the law of nature. Equally Lutheranism has witnessed repeated attempts throughout its history, by the pietists, by the upholders of the collegiate theory of the Church and by the Confessional Church in the twentieth century, to free the Church from the domination of the State and to allow it to make full and free use of the rich inheritance in liturgy, scripture and life which Luther bequeathed to it. If there has been no final solution as to the true nature of the Lutheran Church, this is in no way surprising since it has continued to bear the marks of the paradoxical personality of the great man who gave it its generally-accepted name.

CHAPTER 10

Epilogue

Although Luther's influence rather than his powers diminished towards the end of his life, he had become something of a legend in his own life-time. It was in some sense as a myth that successive ages treated his personality and work. In his opening chapter to his judicious and penetrating study, *The Righteousness of God*, the distinguished English Lutheran scholar, Gordon Rupp, has outlined the fascinating historiography of Luther. The first generation of Lutherans regarded him as the *Wundermann*, the man who had been sent by and called by God, the 'veritable Elijah and a John the Baptist, whom God has sent before the Great Day' as Coelius described him. In his *Historia Lutheranismi* the seventeenth-century writer, von Seckendorf, perceived God as well as Luther at work in the Reformation, '*agente Luthero, sed et hoc dirigente Deo*'. A more critical attitude developed towards the end of the seventeenth century, 'though I rate

Luther highly, I recognise he was a man', Philip Spener commented, 'and I rate him far, far below the Apostles'. Uncritical hero-worship tended to be succeeded by partisan biography, dictated by the writer's own historical or theological presuppositions. Luther for Leibnitz was the champion of conscience. Johann Semlar in the eighteenth century christened him the prophet of the enlightenment. Lessing saw in his career the liberator from outworn tradition and religious enslavement. Justus Möser believed him to be the peaceful preacher of the true Gospel. Frederick the Great of Prussia, unsympathetic towards his religious enthusiasm, appreciated his German patriotism.

Indeed, with the emergence of a German political philosophy in which national feeling was deeply ingrained, Luther became the epitome of the national spirit. 'Luther', the poet Herder observed somewhat curiously, 'Simply, unlettered Luther, how dear was the Word of God to you . . . thou shouldest be living at this hour, Germans have need of thee.' It was during the celebration of the three-hundredth anniversary of the posting of the 95 theses in 1817 that the students from Jena University flocked to the Wartburg Castle and thrust reactionary books and other symbols of military conservatism into the flames of a bonfire. Mendelssohn wrote a 'Reformation' Symphony. Luther became a prophet of the new German nationalism. Even in the mid-twentieth century the apparent Erastianism of his politics and his fierce attacks on the Jews proved sufficient to foster the view that he was one of the architects of modern Germany.

Early Roman Catholic interpretations were understandably hostile. Luther had denounced the Pope, apostasised from his vows and married a runaway nun. His character, it was thought, could only be ultimately explained in terms of diabolic possession. His mother, it was suggested but without an iota of evidence, was a public-bath attendant who had been seduced by a demon. There was a wild look in his eyes (and indeed contemporaries noted the peculiar intensity of his eyes, their flashing, almost hypnotic brilliance) which denoted secret communion with a devil. His death was variously interpreted. He committed suicide and demons snatched his corpse from the coffin in the funeral procession. He had died as a result of a drunken bout in bed with a nun. The Franciscan, John Nas, a reclaimed Lutheran convert from Catholicism, provoked by the Protestant court chaplain's frankly entitled tract 'One Hundred, Select, Great, Shameless, Fat, Well-Swilled, Stinking, Papistical Lies' turned gleefully to depict the 'Anatomy of Lutheranism as it was instituted by the Devil'.

The evidence which Denifle presented was certainly impressive

Siebenköpffe Martini Luthers
Vom Hochwürdigen Sacrament des Altars / Durch
Doctor Jo. Cocleus.

Doctor · Martinus · Luther · Ecclesiast · Schwirmer · Visitier · Barrabas

Martinus Luther
Siebenkopff.

35 Luther depicted as a seven-headed monster
From Bainton, 'Here I Stand', Abingdon Press

and his influence on anti-Lutheran writers has been continuous and considerable; but it had been marshalled in a distinctly slanted fashion. He had, for instance, laid great stress on Luther's use of the word '*concupiscentia*', mistakeningly interpreting it as sexual lust. He quoted a phrase which Luther used in a letter to his wife, 'I gorge myself like a Bohemian and I get drunk like a German. God be praised. Amen', to suggest that he was a worldly man, but he did not note the context of the letter, a humorous one written to his wife when she was very worried by his poor appetite. He used a series of portraits in his first edition to show how the thin, ascetic scholar and monk became obese and unattractive; the last of his portraits, he noted, was 'surprisingly bestial', though the fact that it was made of the reformer after his death, and possibly after decomposition had set in, should have minimised his astonishment.

Although Denifle's insistence that there was a fundamental moral flaw in his personality was questioned by the scholarly Jesuit, Hartmann Grisar, yet his interpretation of Luther was not basically different. 'The real origin of Luther's teaching', he concluded, 'must be sought in a fundamental principle . . . his unfavourable estimate of good works'. While other pejorative estimates of Luther's character and work, as those of Maritain and Weijenborg, have been published, recent Catholic historians, such as Gilson, Vignaux and Johann Lortz, have shewn a scholarly understanding of the man and his theology.

In fact a revolution in Luther studies occurred in the last century, culminating in a profound reappraisal of his importance in the course of the twentieth century, and caused a virtual renaissance of Lutheran studies which is still in full flood. Through Schleiermacher, Theodosius and Adolf Harnack, Troeltsch, Karl Holl, perhaps the most distinguished representative of German Lutheran scholarship, Franz Lau, Boehmer, Bornkamm, Nathan Soderblom and Einar Billing, a determined effort has been made by German and Scandinavian scholars to evaluate Luther's importance and to ascertain the features of his personality and thought. The movement has evoked penetrating textual studies and varied but learned discussions on Lutheran theology. It has demonstrated conclusively Luther's greatness and thrown much light on his significance, more, perhaps, by way of the development of his theology than by reason of his place in the history of the sixteenth century: this is hardly surprising since the revival of Lutheran studies sprang in part from the decline of liberal theology and the rise of the 'dialectical' school of Karl Barth. 'May we speak', Gordon Rupp has written, 'after the motif research of the Scandinavians, of a

195

coherent centre of Luther's theology, or is it, as Lortz supposes, a tumultuous, genial, inchoate flood? May we speak with the Swedish theologians, Anders Nygren, of Luther's Copernican Revolution, his substitution of a God-centred doctrine of redemption for the man-centred theology of the late Middle Ages? Or, with the Danish theologian, Regin Prenter, of Luther's return to the Biblical realism, of personal encounter with God, in contrast to the medieval and Augustinian doctrines of infused charity? Or, with the Finnish scholar, Lennart Pinomaa, of the break through of Luther from formal and academic notions to a genuinely 'existential' theology relating to thought and life?'[1]

In spite of the immense literature that now exists about Martin Luther, perhaps because of it, elements of confusion and uncertainty must remain. There persist baffling features in his personality, inconsistencies and paradoxes, which have aroused the interest of the psychologist[2] but which still defy solution. The extent to which Luther's success depended upon the favourable conditions of his time must remain a matter of debate. The degree of incoherence and inconsistency in his own thought is not easy to establish; nor is the final significance of his work as a systematic theologian. Even the actual historical importance of the Reformation may well be challenged. It can certainly be argued that it was the last of the medieval religious movements, and that Luther and his opponents had much more in common than was for long supposed. The future lay with more radically-minded thinkers who were to emerge from the changing conditions brought into being by the economic, social and religious movements of Luther's day.

Yet, taking all this into account, a reckoning can be made. Whether the premisses upon which he founded his faith and life were fallacious or not, there can be no doubt that Luther was a many-sided genius whose creative energy was ultimately more impressive than his destructive fury. Although the authenticity of some of his work, especially the *Table Talk*, founded on reportage, may be challenged, there is enough in the projected 94 folio volumes of the Weimar edition to demonstrate the depth, range and height of his theology. His personality was prophetic with all the defects as well as the virtues of

[1] Gordon Rupp, *Luther's Progress to the Diet of Worms* (1951), 103.
[2] Preserved Smith first followed this approach in an article in the *American Journal of Psychology* in 1913. The most authoritative study is Dr. J. P. Reiter, *Martin Luthers Umwelt, Charakter und Psychose* (1937–41). Cf. also E. Erikson, *Young Man Luther* (1959).

the prophet. Profound emotion and spiritual sensitivity combined with penetrating judgment, deep biblical scholarship and intellectual power to make him the most prominent spiritual leader of his time. His mind was perhaps less incisive and his administrative genius less marked than that of John Calvin, and his general outlook more old-fashioned. In the long run Calvinism exerted greater influence over the future history of the world, but conservative revolutionary as he may well have been, Luther more than any one person fractured the unity of medieval Christendom and challenged the authority of the Church. 'He came', in Lortz' words, 'to stand outside the Church without intending to do so.' Even given the circumstances which made his life's work possible, few men have left such an impression on the history of their day, and it is certain that we shall not see his like again.

The Main Events in Luther's Life

1483	Born at Eisleben
1501–5	At the University of Erfurt
1502	Foundation of the University of Wittenberg
1505	Became an Augustinian Friar
1507	Ordained to the priesthood.
1508	Lectured at Wittenberg
1510	Visited Rome
1511	Became a professor at Wittenberg
1513–15	Lectured on the Psalms
1515–16	Lectured on Romans
1516–17	Lectured on Galatians
1517–18	Lectured on Hebrews
1517	Attacked indulgences in the 95 theses
1518	Interview with Cardinal Cajetan at Augsburg
1519	Dispute with Eck at Leipzig
	Charles V elected Holy Roman Emperor
1520	Publication of the *Address to the German Nobility*; the *Babylonian Captivity of the Church*; the *Freedom of a Christian Man*
	Papal Bull *Exsurge Domine* condemned Luther's heresies
1521	Papal Bull *Decet Romanum Pontificem* excommunicated Luther
	Diet and Edict of Worms
	Death of Pope Leo X
1521–2	Luther at the Wartburg Castle
1522	Adrian VI elected Pope
	The Knights' War
	Luther completed the translation of the N.T. into German
	Luther returned to Wittenberg
1523	Clement VII elected Pope
1524	Luther abandoned his religious habit

198

1524–5	The Peasants' War
1525	Luther married Katharine von Bora
	Luther in dispute with Erasmus
	Frederick the Wise of Saxony succeeded by his brother, John
1526	Diet and Recess of Speyer
1529	Protestation of Speyer
	Siege of Vienna by the Turks
	Colloquy of Marburg
	Luther published *Greater* and *Smaller Catechism*
1530	Diet and Confession of Augsburg
1531	Zwingli killed at Kappel
	Formation of the Schmalkaldic League
1532	Religious Peace of Nuremberg
	Elector John of Saxony succeeded by John Frederick
1534	Luther completed translation of the O.T. into German
	Paul III elected Pope
	Anabaptist rising in Münster
1536	Wittenberg Concord
	Calvin in Geneva
1537	Schmalkaldic Articles published
1539	Bigamous marriage of Philip of Hesse
1541	Religious Colloquy of Ratisbon
1544	Diet of Speyer
	Peace of Crépy between Charles V and Francis I
1545	Opening of the Council of Trent
1546	Luther died
	The Schmalkaldic War
1547	Battle of Mühlberg
1548	The *Interim* of Augsburg
1555	The Religious Peace of Augsburg
	Abdication of the Emperor Charles V

Books for Further Reading

There is an immense literature in German: see the annual bibliographies in the *Luther-Jahrbuch* and K. Aland, *Hilfsbuch zum Lutherstudium*, 2nd ed. (1958). The standard edition of his works is the *Weimarer Ausgabe*, Weimar, (1883 ff). See also H. S. Grimm, 'Luther Research since 1920', in *The Journal of Modern History*, XXXII (1960), 105–18.

An American edition of Luther's work in 55 volumes is projected; 21 volumes, ed. Jaroslav Pelikan and H. T. Lehmann (1955 ff), have so far appeared, including two which cover the main events of Luther's career. Other translations of his main works in English include: *Primary Works*, ed. H. Wace and C. A. Buchheim (1896); *The Precious and Sacred Writings* of Martin Luther, ed. J. N. Lenker, 14 vols. (1903–10); *Selected Letters*, ed. M. A. Currie (1908); *Luther's Correspondence*, 2 vols., ed. Preserved Smith and C. M. Jacobs (1913–18); *Conversations with Luther*, ed. Preserved Smith and H. P. Gallinger (1915); *A Compend of Luther's Theology*, ed. H. T. Kerr (1943); *Reformation Writings of Martin Luther*, 2 vols., ed. B. L. Woolf (1952–6); *Commentary on Galatians*, ed. P. S. Watson (1953); *Letters of Spiritual Counsel*, ed. T. G. Tapport (1955); *On the Bondage of the Will*, ed. J. I. Packer and O. R. Johnston (1957); *Lectures on Romans*, W. Pauck (1961); *Luther; Early Theological Works*, ed. J. Atkinson (1962).

General histories of the Reformation include: T. M. Lindsay, *A History of the Reformation*, 2 vols. (1906–7); J. P. Whitney, *The Reformation* (1907; new ed., 1940); A. Plummer, *The Continental Reformation* (1912); Preserved Smith, *The Age of the Reformation* (1921); N. Sykes, *The Crisis of the Reformation* (1939); J. Mackinnon, *The Origins of the Reformation* (1939); V. H. H. Green, *Renaissance and Reformation* (1951); H. J. Grimm, *The Reformation Era* (1954); R. H. Bainton, *The Reformation of the Sixteenth Century* (1952); Will Durant, *The Reformation* (1957). See also B. J. Kidd, *Documents*

Illustrative of the Continental Reformation (1911); R. Pascal, *The Social Basis of the German Reformation* (1933); H. Holborn, *Ulrich von Hutten and the German Reformation* (1937); J. P. Whitney, *Reformation Essays* (1939); *The New Cambridge Modern History*, Vol. II, ed. G. R. Elton (1958); K. Holl, *The Cultural Significance of the Reformation*, trans. Hertz and Lichtblau (1959); S. A. Fischer-Galati, *Ottoman Imperialism and German Protestantism* (1959) and G. H. Williams, *The Radical Reformation* (1962).

The chief biographies of Luther in English are: H. Grisar (Eng. trans. 6 vols., 1913–17); A. C. McGiffert (1911); C. Beard, *Luther and the Reformation in Germany until the Close of the Diet of Worms*, ed. J. F. Smith, 1889; J. Mackinnon, *Luther and the Reformation*, 4 vols. (1925–30); L. P. V. Febvre (1930); F. Funck-Brentano (1936); H. Boehmer, *Martin Luther; Road to Reformation* (trans. 1957); R. H. Bainton, *Here I Stand* (1951); E. G. Schwiebert, *Luther and his Times* (1950); E. G. Rupp, *Luther's Progress to the Diet of Worms* (1951); R. H. Fife, *The Revolt of Martin Luther* (1957); G. Ritter, *Luther*, trans. J. Riches (1963).

On his theology and thought see: J. Kostlin, *Luther's Theology* (2 vols., 1897); H. Boehmer, *Luther in Light of Recent Research* (1936); C. M. Carlson, *The Reinterpretation of Luther* (1948); H. H. Kramm, *The Theology of Martin Luther* (1947); P. S. Watson, *Let God be God!* (1947); R. E. Davies, *The Problem of Authority in the Continental Reformers* (1946); M. Reu, *Luther's German Bible* (1934); M. Reu, *Luther and the Scriptures* (1944); E. G. Rupp, *The Righteousness of God* (1953); Regin Prenter, *Spiritus Creator, Studies in Luther's Theology* (1953); W. A. Mueller, *Church and State in Luther and Calvin* (1954); J. Dillenberger, *God Hidden and Revealed* (1953); H. Bornkamm, *Luther's World of Thought* (1958); F. E. Cranz, *Development of Luther's Thought on Justice, Law and Society* (1959); A. S. Wood, *Luther's Principle of Biblical Interpretation* (1960); B. A. Gerrish, *Grace and Reason* (1962); T. M. McDonough, *The Law and the Gospel of Luther* (1963); W. Pauck, *The Heritage of the Reformation* (1950); E. W. Zeeden, *The Legacy of Luther* (1954).

Index

The numerals in **bold** type refer to the figure numbers of the illustrations